The 25 Greatest Achievements in Golf

The Best of the Best

BY TOM WATSON AND SANDY TATUM

With Martin Davis

Edited by Desmond Tolhurst

THE AMERICAN GOLFER

Greenwich

$\mathscr{The}$ American Golfer

American Golfer titles may be purchased for business or promotional use or for special sales.
For information, please write to: The American Golfer, Inc., 151 Railroad Avenue, Greenwich,
Connecticut 06830.

FIRST EDITION

ISBN 1-57243-247-0

Published by:

The American Golfer, Inc.
151 Railroad Avenue
Greenwich, Connecticut 06830
(203) 862-9720
Fax (203) 862-9724

Design by:

ALL CAPS
599 Riverside Avenue
Westport, Connecticut 06880
(203) 221-1609

Co-published by:

Triumph Books
644 South Clark Street
Chicago, Illinois 60605

Distributed to the golf trade by:

The Booklegger
13100 Grass Valley Avenue
Grass Valley, California 95945

ACKNOWLEDGEMENTS

We wish to express our sincerest appreciation to the primary authors of this book, Tom Watson
and Sandy Tatum.

A very special thanks to John Morris of the PGA TOUR for his fine copy editing; to Desmond
Tolhurst for his invaluable editorial input, fact-checking and general assistance; and to Carol Petro
of ALL CAPS for her marvelous art direction. This book could not have been published without
their active assistance and cooperation.

Several organizations and individuals were responsible for providing many of the original
photographs appearing in this book: specifically Brett Avery and Maxine Vigliotta of the United
States Golf Association, the PGA TOUR, Joe Steranka of the PGA of America, Brian Morgan,
the Associated Press, Matt Lawrence of Famous Photography, The Bettmann Archive, Frank
Christian Studios, *Golf Digest*, *Golfworld*, *The New York Times*, *The Miami Herald*, *The Seattle
Daily Times*, *The Knoxville News-Sentinel*, *Greensboro News & Record*, *The (*Montreal) *Gazette*,
The Spokesman-Review, Thornhill Country Club and Hope Valley Country Club.

And last, but certainly not least, thanks to MasterCard for allowing us to produce this book.

This book is dedicated to the memory of Ben Hogan,
whose approach to the playing of the game took golf to another level.

Table of Contents

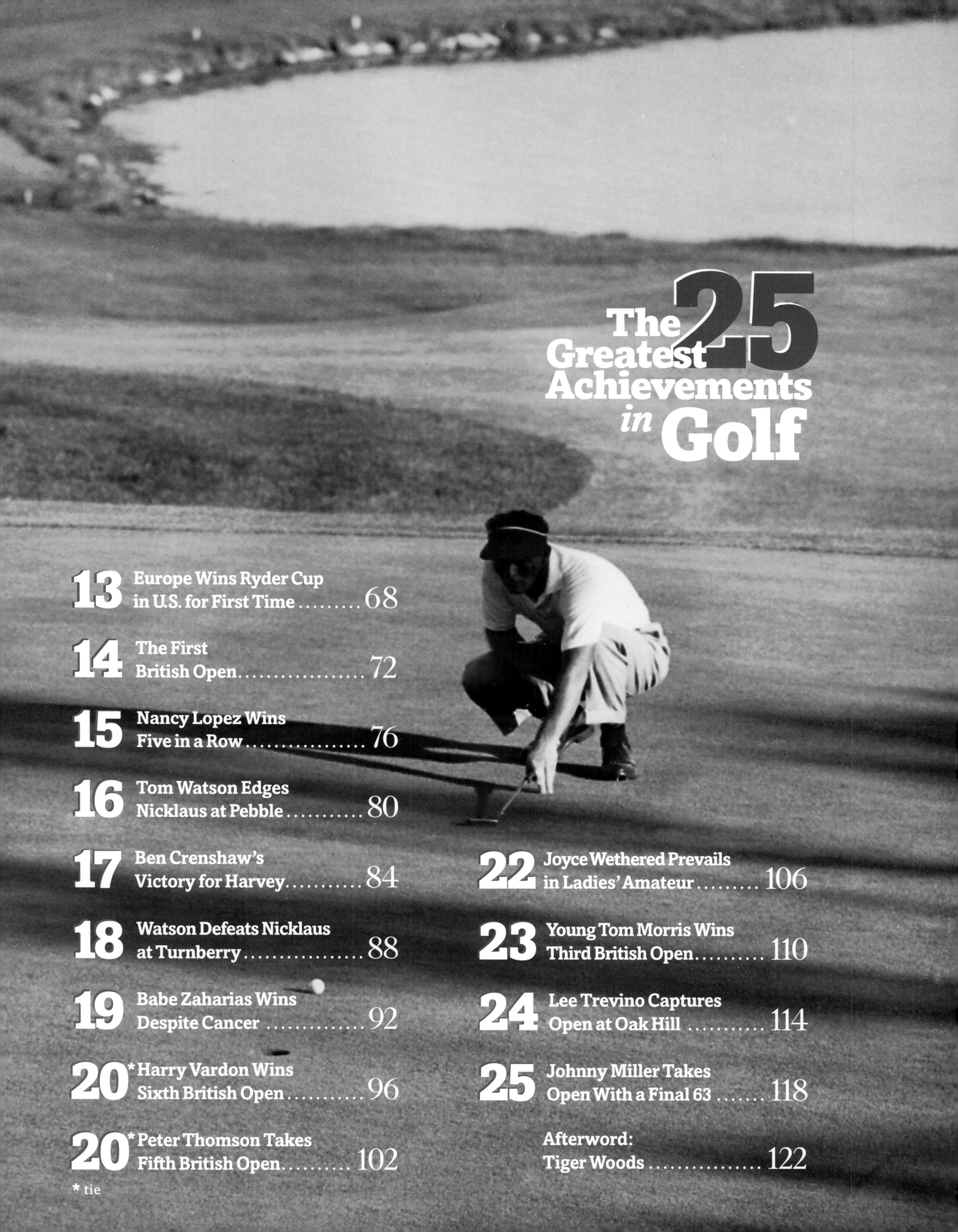

The 25 Greatest Achievements *in* Golf

* tie

Ann Laird (left) and Mary Black (right), Bobby Jones' granddaughters, with Alan Heuer, president of MasterCard.

Searching for the Best of the Best

RECOGNIZING THE 25 GREATEST ACHIEVEMENTS in golf history—and honoring the people who contributed so much to the lore of the game through those accomplishments—were the reasons that the PGA TOUR and MasterCard International decided to conduct a search for "The Best of the Best in Golf."

Gene Lockhart (then the CEO of MasterCard) and I had discussed ways in which MasterCard could extend its involvement in golf beyond the sponsorship of events and into promotion of the game and its values. When MasterCard asked Tom Watson to be the spokesman for its golf interests, it became clear to the three of us—Gene, Tom and myself—that a search for golf's defining moments would be a way to contribute to the public appreciation of the game's history and traditions.

Tom, who has contributed so much to the history of the game as a player, asked his friend, Frank D. "Sandy" Tatum, to serve as Chairman of a Select Committee that would sift through the archives of the game and compile a list of 25 great achievements in golf, milestones in the wonderful lore of the game.

Sandy, a former president of the USGA and one of the game's great ambassadors, formed a committee that included people from all of golf's fairways and byways. The Select Committee compiled the list that is included in this publication.

The daunting task of ranking the 25 great golf achievements in the order of their significance was turned over to the International Voting Body for the World Golf Hall of Fame, which determined the final order of these great benchmark accomplishments in golf.

As is true with any ranking, each of us may have our own opinion on the game's greatest moments; but the reason for compiling this list remains the same—to recognize the people and deeds who have helped deliver the game to us in its present healthy state and have helped ensure its bright future.

Timothy W. Finchem
Commissioner
PGA TOUR

Foreword

THE CONCEPT FOR THIS BOOK, *The 25 Greatest Achievements in Golf*, had its genesis in 1996 when MasterCard and the PGA TOUR decided it would be especially interesting to identify what they called "The Best of the Best in Golf"—the most memorable moment in golf's history.

A Select Committee was organized, which assembled an impressive cumulative knowledge of the history of golf. I had the honor of serving as Chairman of this Committee, whose composition is identified below:

The Select Committee

Frank D. Tatum, Jr. (Chairman)
Past president, USGA

Ruffin Beckwith
Executive Director, World Golf Village

Peggy Kirk Bell
Owner, Pine Needles Resort and Teaching Center

Michael Bonallack
Secretary, Royal and Ancient Golf Club of St. Andrews

Alistair Cooke
Author/commentator

Thomas L. Crow
Former Australian Amateur champion

Larry Dorman
*Golf writer, The New York Times;
President, Golf Writers Association of America*

Maureen Garrett
Former president, Ladies' Golf Union of Great Britain

Bob Green
Retired golf writer, Associated Press

John Hopkins
Golf writer, The Times of London

Sadao Iwata
Commentator/writer, Tokyo Sports Press

Dan Jenkins
Golf writer, Golf Digest

Jim Murray
Columnist, Los Angeles Times

George Peper
Editor, Golf Magazine

Betsy Rawls
LPGA Hall of Fame, tournament director

Our task was to identify 25 "moments" that would qualify for consideration in determining which was the greatest.

Our committee decided that a more fitting description of our quest was "outstanding achievement." In this way, we would consider everything from a single shot to a single season to an entire career for the final list of 25 nominees as the greatest moment in golf history.

The Select Committee's list of 25 then went to the international voting body for the World Golf Hall of Fame, which made the final choices for "MasterCard's Best of the Best in Golf." The results were announced during the MasterCard Championship in Hualalai, Hawaii, in January 1997.

Involvement in this process stimulated the thought that those 25 achievements going back to 1744 provide perhaps the most interesting way of expressing the history of the game of golf. This book, therefore, is the ultimate result.

I should note that there have been so many singular achievements (the Committee's first list added up to 115!), that attempting to confine them to 25 has to be both a subjective and a more or less arbitrary judgment.

The 25 achievements featured in this book—presented in the order they finished in the voting, certainly do illustrate how incredibly rich is the history of this singular game.

A distinctive feature of these 25 achievements is the character of the people who achieved them:

Bobby Jones	Arnold Palmer	Peter Thomson
Jack Nicklaus	Nancy Lopez	Joyce Wethered
Byron Nelson	Tom Watson	Young Tom Morris
Francis Ouimet	Ben Crenshaw	Lee Trevino
Ben Hogan	Babe Zaharias	Johnny Miller
Gene Sarazen	Harry Vardon	

Consideration of that list identifies how distinctive—individually and collectively—these people are. If a like process so evaluated any other area of human endeavor, I would wager that those so identified could not come close to matching this group in terms of consistency of impressive character.

This group, furthermore, identifies a core feature of the game of golf. It takes character to play it properly. It takes exceptional character to be preeminent.

There are those, moreover, who assert that there is something more than that involved; that there are values and related experiences in the playing of the game that take the game into another realm. Michael Murphy's *Golf in the Kingdom* provides a case in point.

The evolution of the game does have elements of mystique. Consider, for example, that the governance of a game with so much commercial potential emanated from a private amateur golf club located on the northeast coast of Scotland. Two hundred and fifty-plus years later, as the game developed around the world and spawned a multibillion-dollar industry, that private amateur golf club continues to govern the game wherever it is played, excepting only in the United States and Mexico. Those countries, moreover, essentially adopted the rules promulgated by that private golf club.

It is understandable, therefore, that people who write about golf's history are prone to resort to metaphysics.

Witness Alistair Cooke's commentary in a foreword to a Sir Guy Campbell tour de force on the history of golf:

"Sir Guy Campbell's classic account of the formation of the links beginning with Genesis and moving step by step to the thrilling arrival of "Tilth" on the fingers of coastal land, suggests that such notable features of our planet as dinosaurs, the prairies, the Himalayas, the seagull, the female of the species herself, were accidental by-products of the Almighty's preoccupation with the creation of the old course at St. Andrew's."

However the development of golf's values and experiences may be explained, there can be no doubt that in the entire history of the human race there never has been, nor ever will be, another game that has so much to offer those who take to it.

—*Sandy Tatum*

1

1930: Bobby Jones and the Grand Slam

The British Amateur

"UNIQUE" IS THE ONLY WORD THAT DESCRIBES both the Grand Slam of 1930 and Bobby Jones, the man who achieved it. In that single year, he won the four major championships of his era, the British Amateur, the British Open, the U. S. Open and the U. S. Amateur. Unique means "one of a kind"—no ifs, ands or buts, or qualifications of any kind. The feat and the man were unique and remain unique to this day.

Jones had a distressing start in life. Born March 17, 1902, he had a digestive ailment doctors considered near hopeless. In fact, they did not expect him to survive infancy. Nonetheless, he did survive and, at the age of five, took up golf. He soon showed a natural genius for the game. At age 11, he shot 80 on a 6,500-yard course. At 14, he was a strong, stocky lad who could drive the ball 250 yards. That year, 1916, he entered his first U. S. Amateur at Merion. He went to the quarterfinals, losing to the defending champion, Bob Gardner.

His health had recovered, but throughout his youth he suffered from an explosive temper that, at times, was uncontrollable. Emotional demons had him throwing and breaking clubs. Somehow he managed to overcome these demons and become one of the most gracious and charming sportsmen ever to have played any game.

He won his first major championship, the U. S. Open, in 1923 at age 21. In the next six years, he won two more U. S. Opens (and finished second in three others), two British Opens and four U. S. Amateurs. From 1923 through 1930, he played in only seven events other than these majors and won four of them.

But 1930 would be the most memorable year in all of golf history.

First there was the British Amateur at St. Andrews. Up to that time, this was the only major championship he had not won. He took care of that by winning seven matches, two of them on the last green.

As burly Scottish policemen escorted Jones back to the clubhouse through the excited crowd, O. B. Keeler, Jones' biographer, finally reached him. Jones said, "Honestly, O. B., I don't care what happens now. I'd rather have won this championship than anything else in golf." However Jones may then have felt, what then happened transcended anything ever done before or since in golf.

A victorious Jones being escorted back to the R & A clubhouse after the final round match with Roger Wethered.

Inset: *Col. Skene of the R & A presents the Amateur trophy to Bob Jones.*

1

1930: Bobby Jones and the Grand Slam

The British Open

After his victory in the British Amateur, Bobby Jones went on to Hoylake, where he won his third British Open championship. After two rounds, Jones had a one-stroke lead on rounds of 70, two under par, and 72. Despite a struggle on the last day—he shot 74, 75 for a total of 291—he beat Leo Diegel and Mac Smith by two shots.

He won despite a ghastly lapse on the par-five eighth hole in the final round. His third shot, a chip, failed to reach the green. His second chip was also weak, leaving him 10 feet short. He then three-putted for a double bogey 7. As Bernard Darwin said in *The Times*, "A nice old lady with a croquet mallet could have saved Jones two strokes."

Bob Jones drives from the tee at Hoylake.

Above: *Jones receives the ancient claret jug, emblematic of victory in the British Open, from the Captain of the Hoylake Golf Club.*

1
1930: Bobby Jones and the Grand Slam

The U.S. Open

On July 2, New York honored Bobby Jones with the second ticker-tape parade of his career. Eight days later, he was playing his first round in the U.S. Open at the Interlachen Country Club in Minnesota. The heat was sweltering—the temperature over 95 degrees in the shade, with near matching humidity. Jones managed a one-under-par 71, one stroke behind the leaders. Thankfully, the heat and humidity moderated on the second day, and Jones had a 73, two strokes off the pace.

In the third round, Jones produced a stunning 68 to lead by five. The championship appeared to be his. In the last round, however, his four birdies and 11 pars were more than offset by three double bogeys on par threes. On the last hole, too, Jones narrowly avoided disaster. He had underclubbed on his second shot, leaving the ball 40 feet short of the hole—three-putt territory. But, as he so often did in the clutch, he then holed the putt for the winning birdie, scoring 75 for a total of 287. Mac Smith was second, only two strokes behind.

This Open was the first to be broadcast live on radio. For two hours, Ted Husing, using a portable transmitter and microphone, reported from the 17th and 18th greens for the Columbia Broadcasting System. That afternoon, 20 runners brought him the scores through a gallery of 15,000.

Above: *New York feted Jones with a ticker-tape parade on his return from Britain.*

Left: *Bob Jones pitches from the fringe at the 485-yard, par-5 eighth hole at Interlachen after it skipped across the surface of the pond fronting the green on his second shot. Considered Jones' luckiest shot in tournament golf, he went on to birdie the hole and win his fourth Open.*

1 1930: Bobby Jones and the Grand Slam

U.S. Amateur

The final act of the Grand Slam, the U.S. Amateur, took place at Merion in September.

Bobby Jones utterly dominated that championship. He was medalist, with 69-73—142, equaling the lowest qualifying score for the Amateur. In the final, a gallery of 18,000 watched Jones crush Eugene Homans by 8 and 7.

Two months later, at the age of 28, he retired from competitive golf. He had no more worlds to conquer.

Bobby Jones was the quintessential amateur. His competitive golf was practically confined to the major championships. At home, he averaged only 80 rounds of golf a year. By profession, he was a lawyer, but he also had a degree in mechanical engineering from Georgia Tech and another in English from Harvard. He studied law at Emory Law School, but left before receiving a degree because he had taken, and passed, the Georgia bar examination.

Sadly, his respite from illness ended at age 46, when he began to suffer from a disease diagnosed in 1956 as syringomylia, a chronic progressive degenerative disease of the spinal cord. For 23 years, until his death at age 69, he dealt with the ravages of this awful sickness with almost superhuman grace and courage while still managing, until near the end, to be the perfect host every spring at the Masters.

Alistair Cooke puts all this into perspective with these thoughts:

"What we are left with in the end is a forever young, good looking Southerner, an impeccably courteous and decent man with a private ironical view of life who, to the great good fortune of people who saw him, happened to play the great game with more magic and more grace than anyone before or since."

The more cogent summing up, however, was provided by his young Scot caddie during a round at St. Andrews who, reacting to a marvelous shot Bobby Jones had played, said, "My, but you are a wonder, Sir."

Homans concedes to Jones on the 11th hole at Merion.

Inset: *Bob Jones with the Grand Slam trophies and Jones chronicler O.B. Keeler of* The Atlanta Constitution.

2

Jack Nicklaus' Career Achievements

The U.S. Amateur

If one is to judge Jack Nicklaus' career achievements fairly, there is probably no better measure than Jack's own standard, which he once expressed when evaluating the career of Bobby Jones: "The essence of Jones' greatness was that he could play great golf on the great occasions …victories in the major championships are the only ones that really matter."

By this standard, Nicklaus' achievements are staggering. His 18 victories in today's professional majors are far ahead of other great players. The list reads: Jones, 13 majors; Walter Hagen, 11; Ben Hogan and Gary Player, nine; Tom Watson and Arnold Palmer, eight, and Sam Snead and Harry Vardon, seven.

Of course, the earlier players could not play in all the majors as we know them today. Jones, an amateur, who did not play in the PGA, and who himself started the Masters after his retirement, counts four U.S. Amateurs among his 13 majors. When Hagen played in the first Masters in 1934, he was 43, well past his prime. Moreover, in his time, many regarded the Western Open as a major—Hagen won five of them! For Vardon, the Masters was well before his time, he never played in the PGA and competed in just three U.S. Opens.

If you include the U.S. Amateur, and Jack certainly does, Nicklaus' 20 majors consist of two U.S. Amateurs, four U.S. Opens, six Masters, three British Opens and five PGA Championships.

In 1959, the U.S. Amateur was held at the Broadmoor's East Course in Colorado Springs. Nicklaus' last two matches were the toughest; in the 36-hole semifinals and final against Gene Andrews and Charlie Coe, respectively. He won both by just 1 up. Then 19, he is one of only three to win the title at that age.

Nicklaus' second Amateur victory came in 1961 at Pebble Beach. He put on a marvelous performance, being 20 under par for the 112 holes he played, defeating Dudley Wysong in the final by 8 and 6.

Jack Nicklaus tees off at Pebble Beach during the 1961 U.S. Amateur.
Inset: *Jack with the U.S. Amateur trophy.*

2 Jack Nicklaus' Career Achievements

The U.S. Open

Jack Nicklaus' first professional major came during his first year on the PGA TOUR in the 1962 U.S. Open at Oakmont. Nicklaus shot 72-70-72-69 to tie Arnold Palmer at 283, then won the playoff, 71 to 74.

His second U.S. Open win came at Baltusrol in 1967. His golf was as hot as the blazing weather. He shot 71-67-72-65—275, breaking, by a stroke, the U.S. Open record set by Ben Hogan in 1948 at Riviera. His final-round 65 also tied the Open record.

In 1972 at Pebble Beach, Nicklaus won his third U.S. Open title. In the first three rounds, he shot 71-73-72, even par, for a one-stroke lead. In the last round, Nicklaus' most memorable shot was a 1-iron at 17, which hit the flagstick, stopping just six inches away. He finished in 74 for 290, to win by three from Bruce Crampton.

Nicklaus' fourth U.S. Open win came in 1980 at Baltusrol at a time when many experts said he was finished. After three rounds, he had scored 63-71-70, for 206, tied with Isao Aoki, who had three 68s. In the last round, Nicklaus picked up two strokes early, and never allowed Aoki to get closer than one. Nicklaus shot a final round of 68 for an eight-under 272, to break his own record of 275, set at Baltusrol in 1967. Aoki scored 70 for 274. As the main scoreboard said, "Jack is back!"

Above and Inset: *Jack at the 1972 U.S. Open at Pebble Beach.*

Left: *Jack makes the acceptance speech at the 1980 U.S. Open at Baltusrol. At far left in the front row is former USGA President Jim Hard. Will Nicholson, USGA president, is at Jack's right with Joe Dey, long-time USGA Executive Director and first Commissioner of the PGA TOUR, directly behind Nicholson.*

2 Jack Nicklaus' Career Achievements

The Masters

Jack Nicklaus' first victory in the Masters came in 1963. Opening with a 74, five shots off the lead, Nicklaus then shot 66 to pull within one. During a severe downpour in the third round, he shot a 74 to go into the lead, then edged Tony Lema by one shot with a final-round 72 for 286. At 23, he was the youngest Masters winner.

In 1965, after opening with 67-71, Nicklaus had what he said was "one of the best driving days of my life" and scored 64 in the third round. The longest club Nicklaus used on the par fours was a 6-iron; on the par fives, a 3-iron. A final-round 69 gave him 271, a new four-round record. Bobby Jones said: "Jack is playing a game with which I am not familiar."

Nicklaus successfully defended his Masters title in 1966, scoring 68-76-72-72 to tie Gay Brewer and Tommy Jacobs at 288. In the playoff, Nicklaus and Jacobs both were out in 35; Brewer, 38. At 10 and 11, Nicklaus scored 4-3 to Jacobs' 5-4. These two strokes gave Nicklaus his winning margin. He scored 70; Jacobs, 72; Brewer, 78.

In 1972, Nicklaus tied Arnold Palmer's record of four Masters wins. In the first round, he was two over par after 10 holes; but then birdied 11, 12 and 13, parred 14, eagled 15 and birdied 16 to finish with a 68. After that, he was never seriously threatened, scoring 71-73-74 for 286 to win by three strokes. The low amateur was 20-year-old Ben Crenshaw, in 19th place with 295.

In 1975, Nicklaus won his fifth Masters, his 15th major. After three rounds, Tom Weiskopf led with 207, with Nicklaus one stroke back after rounds of 68-67-73. Johnny Miller was at 211. The shot everyone remembers is Nicklaus' 40-foot putt at the 70th hole, which he holed for a birdie 2 and the lead—and then leaped in the air for joy! His final-round 68 gave him a total of 276. At 18, Miller and Weiskopf both needed birdies to tie, but failed .

In 1986, Nicklaus, at 46, won his sixth Masters and 20th major. Shooting 74-71-69-65—279, Nicklaus came from six shots off the pace to play the last 10 holes in seven under par and win by a stroke from Greg Norman and Tom Kite.

Arnold Palmer helps Jack into the winner's green jacket in 1963.

2 Jack Nicklaus' Career Achievements

The British Open

Jack Nicklaus' first win in the British Open came at Muirfield in 1966. That year, the landing areas for the longer hitters were only about 20 yards wide, and the rough was a foot and half high in places. Nicklaus took irons off the tee most of the time, a winning strategy. He scored 70-67-75-70—282 for a one-stroke victory. Nicklaus had now won all four professional majors, which constitute the modern Grand Slam.

In the 1970 British Open, Nicklaus won at St. Andrews. In the first three rounds, he scored 68-69-73, two strokes back. In the final round, Nicklaus played great golf, but three-putted five times. He scored 72 for 283 to tie Doug Sanders, who missed a three-foot putt on the last hole. Nicklaus won the playoff, 72 to 73.

In 1978, Nicklaus won his third British title, again at St. Andrews. With rounds of 71-72-69-69—281, Nicklaus finished two ahead of Ben Crenshaw, Simon Owen, Ray Floyd and Tom Kite. His win made him the first man to win the majors at least three times each (three U. S. Opens, five Masters, four PGAs and three British).

Jack receives the British Open trophy from the captain of the R&A.

Above: *Jack plays into the wind at the Open.*

23

2 Jack Nicklaus' Career Achievements

The PGA Championship

Jack Nicklaus won his first PGA Championship in 1963 in sweltering heat (100 to 110 degrees) at the Dallas Athletic Club. In the first three rounds, Nicklaus scored 69-73-69—211, three strokes behind Bruce Crampton. In the last round, Nicklaus took a two-stroke lead with a "routine" (for him) birdie at the 543-yard 12th hole—drive, 1-iron, two putts—and a 30-foot birdie putt on 15. He won by the same margin with a 68 for 279.

In 1971, the PGA was played in February—not its regular month, August—at the PGA National Golf Club in Palm Beach Gardens, Florida. Nicklaus shot 69-69-70 in the first three rounds for 208 and a four-stroke lead over Gary Player. In the last round, after four bogeys and a birdie on the first 11 holes, Nicklaus birdied 12 and 17 to score 73 for 281 and win by two strokes over Billy Casper.

In 1973, the PGA was held at the Canterbury Golf Club in Cleveland. Nicklaus was "not happy" with his first-round 72, three strokes behind the leaders. He was happier with his next round, a 68 that left him one back. He then took a one-stroke lead with another 68, and finished with 69 for 277. He won by four strokes over Bruce Crampton. This was Nicklaus' 14th major, to go one ahead of Bob Jones.

In 1975, at the Firestone Country Club in Akron, Ohio, Nicklaus shot a 70 in the first round after missing "a lot of birdie chances." He was three strokes off the lead. In the second round, Crampton shot a record seven-under 63 for the lead at 134. Nicklaus had a "solid" 68 for 138. In the third round, Nicklaus took over with a brilliant 67 for a four-stroke lead. Despite a double bogey at the 72nd hole, he scored 71 for a winning 276. Crampton was second again, two strokes behind.

In the 1980 PGA, Nicklaus demolished Oak Hill, being the only player to finish under par on the Rochester, New York layout revised before the event. After two rounds, Nicklaus was one under par with 70-69, and stood second at 139. Nicklaus raced ahead with a third-round 66; his total of 205 leading by three. His final-round 69 gave him a total of 274, seven strokes ahead of Andy Bean.

Jack in action at the 1975 PGA Championship.

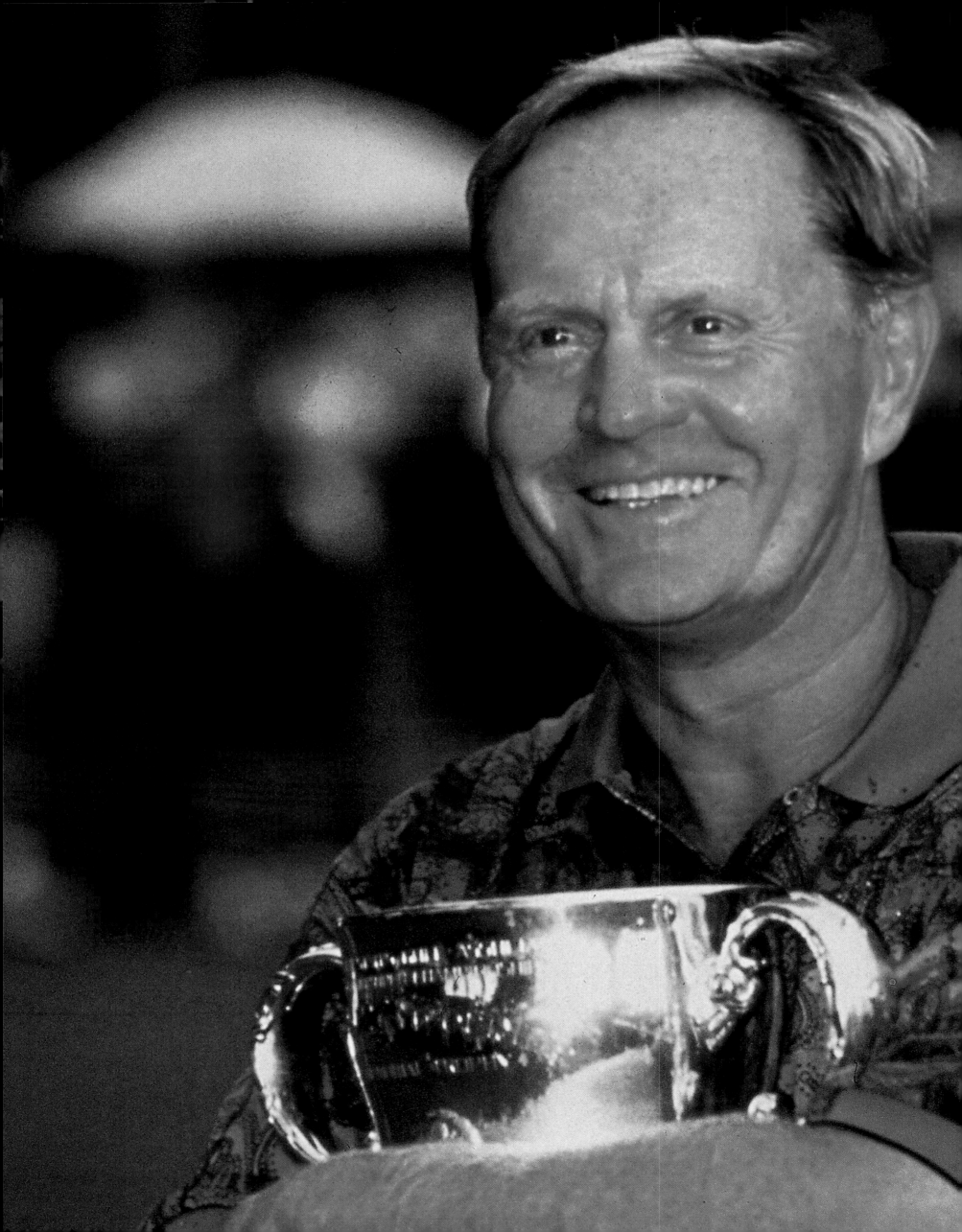

2 Jack Nicklaus' Career Achievements

A striking dimension of Jack Nicklaus' career is its longevity: He won his first U. S. Open in 1962, his last in 1980, 18 years later; his first Masters in 1963, his last in 1986, 23 years later; his first PGA in 1963, his last in 1980, 17 years later.

Another measure of that longevity is his performance in two championships played at Cherry Hills in Denver. The first was in 1960 when, as an amateur, he finished second to Arnold Palmer. In 1993, 33 years later, playing in most respects essentially the same golf course, he won the U.S. Senior Open Championship there with a performance at least as impressive as that he had produced in 1960.

Another dimension is the number of times he has finished second in the majors, 19 in all. A simple list of players who won when he finished second demonstrates how many times he has been in the hunt, as well as the different generations of players he has competed against:

U. S. Open—Arnold Palmer, 1960; Lee Trevino, 1968, 1971; and Tom Watson, 1982.

Masters—Arnold Palmer, 1964; Charlie Coody, 1971; and Tom Watson, 1977, 1981.

British Open—Tony Lema, 1964; Roberto De Vicenzo, 1967; Gary Player, 1968; Lee Trevino, 1972; Johnny Miller, 1976; Tom Watson, 1977; and Seve Ballesteros, 1979.

PGA Championship—Bobby Nichols, 1964; Dave Marr, 1965; Lee Trevino, 1974; and Hal Sutton, 1983.

Even if you judge Nicklaus' record by criteria other than majors, it is awe-inspiring. He has had 70 official PGA TOUR victories, 58 second-place finishes and 36 third-places. Besides his three British Opens, he also has had 11 other international victories, including six Australian Opens and a World Match Play Championship.

There are a number of qualities that have to combine to produce such a stunning record. One of the more easy to identify is Jack's intensity of focus on the shot to be played. That intensity is almost superhuman and rises to a level that ordinary players simply cannot achieve.

There is another quality worth special mention and that is the ability to deal with adversity, indeed disaster, and not let it affect his future play. The 1964 U.S. Open at Congressional provides an interesting example. In the first round, he was well in contention after 15 holes. He then proceeded to miss three short putts, two of them under two feet, in the last three holes. After a solid second round, he missed eight putts of four feet or less in the first seven holes of the third round! That performance would have made a spastic putter out of most ordinary mortals. Jack Nicklaus, however, went on to establish himself as one of the truly great clutch putters ever to play the game.

Comparing players from different eras, with different equipment, different course conditions and different levels of competition is nearly impossible. Nonetheless, there is more than one criterion that seems to identify Jack Nicklaus as perhaps the finest player ever.

Jack won a "senior major," the U.S. Senior Open in 1993.

3

1986: Jack Nicklaus' Sixth Green Jacket at 46

The Masters

IN HIS REPORT ON THE 1986 MASTERS FOR *Golf Digest*, Dan Jenkins put in perspective Jack Nicklaus' winning at Augusta for the sixth time at the age of 46:

"If you want to put golf back on the front pages again and you don't have a Bobby Jones or a Francis Ouimet handy, here's what you do: You send an aging Jack Nicklaus out in the last round of the Masters and let him kill more foreigners than a general named Eisenhower.

"On that final afternoon of the Masters tournament, Nicklaus' deeds were so unexpectedly heroic, dramatic and historic, the taking of his sixth green jacket would certainly rank as the biggest golf story since Jones' Grand Slam of 1930."

At the start of that Masters week, the only attention Jack Nicklaus received was speculation that his career was over. For example, Tom McCollister of *The Atlanta Constitution*, a solid reporter and a veteran of the golf beat, wrote that Nicklaus was "done, through, washed-up and finished."

There were others who thought that McCollister might be right, most notably Jack himself. He had played poorly in 1985, missing the cut in both the U.S. Open and British Open. His performance in 1986 up to the Masters had been even worse. In the eight TOUR events in which he had played, he missed the cut in three, withdrew from a fourth, and could do no better than a tie for 39th place in the remaining four. When he arrived in Augusta, he was 160th on that year's money list with earnings of just $4,404.

Jack had come to the point where he had begun to question whether he should continue playing tournament golf, and had shared these concerns with his family.

There was no doubt about their reaction. "Barbara and the children all definitely wanted me to continue playing," Nicklaus says. While he continued to play, however, he admitted that the question "would be a frequent visitor and, ultimately, almost a constant companion."

Nicklaus started very quietly, for him, with a two-over-par 74. He then played progressively better, shooting a 71 in the second round and a definitely encouraging 69 in the third. His 54-hole total was 214, only four strokes behind the leader, Greg Norman.

After the third round, he was invited into the pressroom. One reporter asked him, "When did you last break 70?" Nicklaus thought for a moment, then replied with a smile, "It's so long ago, I can't remember!"

Capping his historic sixth win at Augusta, Jack made an eagle three with this putt on the 15th hole.

3

1986: Jack Nicklaus' Sixth Green Jacket at 46

Nicklaus' fourth round started quietly. After eight holes, he was just even par for the round and still only two under for the tournament. Walking down the ninth fairway he said to his son, Jackie, who was cad-dying for him, "I have to get myself in gear right now if I'm going to have any chance at all. We really need a birdie here. If we can get off this hole and through nine under par, then we might make something happen."

He made a 12-footer for a birdie on the ninth hole and then, most characteristically, proceeded to make something happen.

On 10, he hit his drive 275 yards, put his iron 25 feet away and holed the putt for a birdie. On 11, his approach was 20 feet from the hole and he holed it for another birdie. On the treacherous 12th, he pulled his tee shot to the front left side of the green, leaving his ball a good 40 yards from the hole. A chip and two putts added up to a bogey. However, at 13, Jack put his drive in Position A, on the flat just to the right of the creek running down the left side. A fine 3-iron put him on the green, and two putts gave him a birdie. Jack played the 14th sensibly, putting his second shot past the hole, the right place to be. He nearly holed the putt, but got his par. At the 15th, Jack hit a great drive, even judged by his standards—straight down the middle and well over 300 yards. His second shot, again with a 3-iron, was Nicklaus at his best—the ball flying high, then dropping softly on the green some 15 feet away. He holed the putt for an eagle 3.

On 16, Jack's second shot almost holed out, landing on the green in the perfect spot, some 20 feet above and to the right of the hole. It checked, then trickled down the slope, missed the cup by a whisker and finished three feet below. He holed the putt for a birdie. At the 17th, Jack hit his drive to the left, into Augusta's light rough. Fortunately, it found a good lie, his short iron put the ball 15 feet left and a little above the hole and he holed it for yet another birdie.

He was now nine under par and leading the tournament. At the last hole, Jack hit another great drive, fading it just enough to avoid the fairway bunker. But his second shot, with a 6-iron, was not nearly enough club. The hole was cut at the back of the green and he faced an uphill putt of some 50 feet. He had to make par to retain his advantage.

There was never a doubt! He struck the putt perfectly, the ball rolling right up the slope and finishing a scant six inches short. A few moments later, Jack had his par and his winning total of 279.

The man Tom McCollister had written off as "washed up" had played the last 10 holes in seven under par. He had come from six shots behind to win by a stroke. At age 46, he had won his sixth Masters, exactly 23 years after he had won his first.

At the 72nd hole, the Masters gallery let Nicklaus know, in no uncertain terms, its heartfelt appreciation of his unique feat.

"I will never forget the ovation we received on our walk up to the 18th green that day," he later said. "It was deafening, stunning, unbelievable in every way. Tears kept coming to my eyes, and I had to tell myself a num-ber of times to hold back my emotions, that I still had some golf to play."

Jack at the awards presentation ceremony with 1985 Masters winner Bernhard Langer.

Phoenix Open

Corpus Christi Open

New Orleans Open

Miami Four-Ball

PHOTOS: USGA/AP

4

1945: Byron Nelson's Record Year

18 Total Victories—11 in a Row!

THE AXIOM THAT RECORDS ARE MADE TO BE broken does not apply to this record of winning 11 PGA TOUR events in a row in 1945.

"The Streak," as it is often called, is only part of the Byron Nelson story in 1945. His record that year approaches unbelievable when one considers that he closed out the season with a total of 18 TOUR victories. This is another all-time record that now, over 50 years later, also appears untouchable.

That record obviously needs no embellishment. Some elements of it, however, may serve to put it into proper perspective:

▶ In that year, Byron played in 30 official events. He finished first in 18 and second in seven.

▶ His stroke average in those 30 tournaments was 68.33, still the lowest stroke average for a single year.

▶ His last-round stroke average was 67.88.

▶ His stroke average during "The Streak" was 67.45.

▶ His final-round stroke average in "The Streak" was 66.67.

▶ He recorded nearly 100 sub-par rounds, the lowest a 62.

▶ He set a TOUR record for the lowest 72-hole score at the Seattle Open, shooting 62-68-63-66—259.

Those are awesome figures, whether you're talking 1940s or 1990s.

It is true that a few so-called golf experts have tended to downgrade Nelson's achievements in the war years, and especially, of course, in 1945. Because so many players at the time were in the armed services,

Byron comes out of the sand en route to victory No. 10 in the Philadelphia Inquirer Open.

Charlotte Open

Greensboro Open

Durham Open

Atlanta Open

Montreal Open

Philadelphia Open

Chicago Victory

45 PGA

Tam O'Shanter

Canadian Open

4 1945: Byron Nelson's Record Year

they say, he didn't play against top competition. This criticism was perhaps somewhat justified in regard to 1944, but not really in 1945.

During that era, the three finest players, other than Nelson, were Sam Snead, Ben Hogan and Jimmy Demaret. In 1944, Snead only played in four events, winning two, Hogan played in four events, and Demaret in one. However, in the 30 official events in which Nelson played in 1945, these players were out on TOUR for long periods.

Snead played in 21 of the 30 events, winning six of them, with three coming in a row in February and early March. Hogan played in 11 of the 30 events, winning two of them. It should be noted that Hogan had quickly recovered his pre-war form, winning five events that year. Demaret played in six of the events, but did not register a win.

Obviously, Nelson thoroughly dominated the TOUR in 1945. However, this dominance was not limited to just that year. Because of gas rationing, the TOUR in 1943 had shrunk to a mere four events. But, in 1944, as the tide of battle turned in favor of the Allies, the TOUR put on 23 events. Nelson won eight of them. In 1945, as noted, he won 18 of 30 events. In 1946, Nelson was a serious competitor in just 18 events. He won six of them.

Put these figures together and you find that Nelson won 32 of the 71 tournaments in three years. In baseball terms, he batted .450, winning nearly half of the events he entered. He also was second 13 times and third 10 times. He was in the top five in all but nine events.

Byron recalls his thought process while the streak was evolving: "In 1945, when I started playing well and winning money, I started thinking, 'I can get enough money to buy a ranch.' Then I said to myself, 'Boy, another cow, another acre, another downpayment.'"

He bought his ranch and retired from active competition in 1946 at age 34. No one, however, will ever retire his record.

Byron's victory in the PGA Championship came in the only major contested in 1945.

Knoxville Open

Esmeralda Open

Seattle Open

Glen Garden Invitational

THE BOSTON TRAVELER
AND EVENING HERALD

FINAL EXTRA

BOSTON, SATURDAY, SEPTEMBER 20, 1913.   12 PAGES.   ONE CENT.

G PUTS
O DEATH
UTH END

ames and Husband
Injuries After
Rescued

LS OF HEARING
HE BACKYARD

FRANCIS OUIMET, BOSTON AMATEUR, WINS OPEN GOLF TITLE ON PLAY OFF

After the Greatest Battle in the History of American Golf

Woodland Club's Youthful Star Turns in Card of 72; Vardon Second with 77; Ray Third on 78

A RECORD GALLERY OF 10,000 FOLLOWS PLAYERS

HOW THE BETTING RULED ON PLAY-OFF

FRANCIS OUIMET IN CENTRE, VARDON ON HIS RIGHT AND RAY ON HIS LEFT.

ALLEGED SLAYER
TO FACE TRIAL

All the Golf Experts Give Ouimet Highest Praise for His Superb Game

HOTEL MAN SHOT
BY IRATE HUSBAND

5

1913: Francis Ouimet Defeats Vardon and Ray

The U.S. Open

EFFORTS TO PUT THIS TRIUMPH INTO PROPER perspective have included calling it a Cinderella story. That effort does not do justice to Francis Ouimet's accomplishment, because Cinderella had a considerable assist from a fairy godmother, whereas Francis Ouimet's resources were limited to Ouimet himself, plus, it should be noted, those of his 10-year-old caddie, Eddie Lowery, whose contributions included the following advice as Ouimet was preparing to play the second shot into the green on the 72nd hole, "Keep your eye on the ball and hit it!"

The real elements in Ouimet's accomplishment contained more drama than any fable.

Ouimet was a 20-year-old amateur whose only previous appearances on the then national golf scene had been in two national amateur championships in which he had failed to qualify for matchplay. He lived across the street from The Country Club at Brookline, where the 1913 Open was played. His knowledge of the course had been developed by caddying there. The club rules then prohibited caddies from playing the course so that his playing experience on it was severely limited. The impact of his triumph was intensified by his having prevailed in a playoff over not just two professionals, but over Ted Ray, the 1912 British Open champion, and Harry Vardon who had won five British Opens and one U.S. Open. It was as if some unknown caddie had emerged at Oakmont in 1962 to beat Arnold Palmer and Jack Nicklaus in the playoff for the U.S. Open Championship.

After the first day's play, Vardon and Wilfred Reid led at 147, with Ray third at 149. Ouimet was tied for seventh, with 151. At two o'clock in the morning, it began to rain heavily and the downpour continued for the whole of the second day. In the third round, Vardon slipped to a 78—due to poor putting—and Ray had a 76. Ouimet shot a solid 74 to tie the Englishmen at 225.

In the afternoon, Vardon's putting again let him down, while Ray's short game was not up to his usual standard. They scored a pair of weak 79s for totals of 304. Both were despondent and thought they had no chance of winning. Then, one by one, the Americans failed—Mac Smith

Ouimet (center) with Vardon (left) and Ray.

37

5 1913:
Francis Ouimet Defeats Vardon and Ray

finished with 307, as did Walter Hagen and Jim Barnes. John McDermott was one stroke worse. Only Ouimet was left. Vardon and Ray went out to watch the youngster finish.

Unlike today, the Rules then did not give the player any help in wet conditions. For example, if the ball embedded in the green, the player had to play it as it lay! As Ouimet said of the last round, "A high pitch was dangerous, because the ball would become embedded in the turf."

Ouimet put on an excellent show. He had appeared to be headed for a high number after his outward half; he had gone out in 43, with two 6s on this card. He hadn't helped his chances by taking a bogey 5 at 12. When he reached the 13th tee, he knew that he had play the last six holes in two under par to tie Vardon and Ray.

He got one birdie on the par-3 13th, chipping in from 30 feet. After a routine par on 14, he nearly lost a stroke at 15 when he pushed his second into rough. Then, a fine pitch left him a tap-in for his par. On the 16th, he got his par 3, but had to hole a nine-footer to do it. On the 17th, he put his second 20 feet from the pin. He then holed the downhill, sidehill putt for his second birdie. On the 18th, his approach stayed short of the green, but a chip and a four-foot putt gave him his final par. His final-round score of 79 had tied the Englishmen. They would play off over 18 holes the next day.

Having to play those two champions in a playoff for the Open Championship was no problem for that extraordinary young man. He played with wonderful resolve, going out in 38 and back in 34 for a 72 to prevail over Vardon by five strokes and over Ray by six!

It was a triumph for the ages.

Grantland Rice, one of America's top golf writers, penned a poem to celebrate Ouimet's victory. It's deliciously humorous, yet shows, quite unmistakably, his pride in the young American champion. Here's a sample:

> O Soul of a Stalwart, for history's pages
> If I was a Keats or a Gray,
> I'd tell how, for those of the far, unborn, ages,
> You slipped it to Vardon and Ray;
> I'd sing every stroke of your conquering battle
> Until I was fagged out and faint;
> I'd make you the subject of every child's prattle
> If I was a Keats—but I ain't.

Ouimet went on to a fine amateur career, winning the U.S. Amateur in 1914 and 1931. In 1951, he became the first American Captain of the Royal and Ancient Golf Club of St. Andrews.

A victorious Ouimet with his 10-year-old caddy Eddie Lowery.

Inset: *Ouimet in action.*

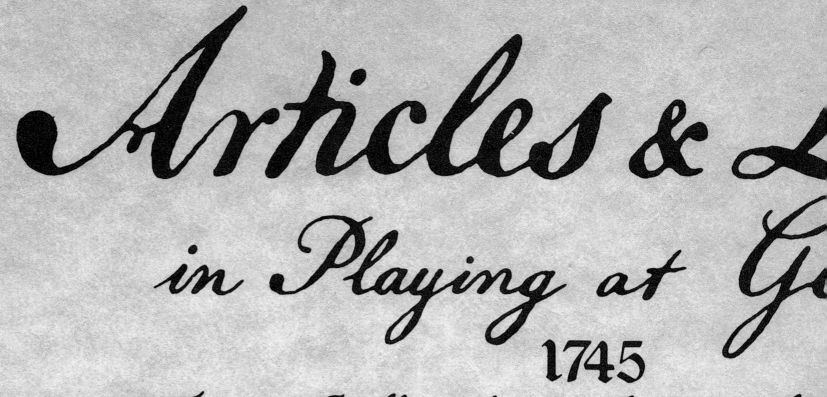

Articles & L

in Playing at G

1745

1. You must Tee your Ball, within a Clubs length o

2. Your Tee must be upon the Ground.

3. You are not to change the Ball which you Strok

4. You are not to remove Stones, Bones or any Bred
   playing your Ball, Except upon the fair Green, with
   your Ball. ————————————————— s that only

5. If your Ball come among Watter or any wattery f
   to take out your Ball & bringing it behind the ha
   may play it with any Club and allow your Adi
   getting out your Ball. —————————

6. If your Balls be found any where touching one
   lift the first Ball till you play the last.

aws

f

he Hole

ff the Tee

Club, for the sake of

a Club's length of

, you are at liberty

rd and Teeing it, you

ary a Stroke, for so

nother, You are to

1744: The First Rules Of Golf

Several Gentlemen of Honour

THE FIRST RULES WERE CREATED FOR A competition held on the first Monday of April 1744, on the Links of Leith. The Gentlemen Golfers of Edinburgh, later the Honourable Company of Edinburgh Golfers, sponsored the event, which, as far as we know, was the first organized golf tournament.

Earlier that year, in March, these golfers, described in the minutes kept by the Magistrates of Edinburgh as "Several Gentlemen of Honour, Skilfull in the ancient and healthfull exercise of the Golf," had petitioned the Magistrates to provide a prize for an annual competition. The Magistrates responded by passing an act which directed their "Treasurer to cause make a SILVER CLUB, not exceeding the value of Fifteen pounds sterling, to be played for annually."

The minutes of that meeting also state that it was to be open for "as many Noblemen or Gentlemen or other Golfers, from any part of Great Britain or Ireland" as should enter. As the tournament was to be open to other than local players, it was necessary to publish the Rules governing the competition.

The meeting further provided that "The Victor (of the competition) shall be called CAPTAIN of the GOLF, and all disputes touching the Golf amongst Golfers, shall be determined by the Captain, and any two or three of the Subscribers."

Thomas Boswall, the captain of The Gentlemen Golfers of Edinburgh, added the following note: "The 5th and 13th Articles of the foregoing Laws having occasioned frequent Disputes it is found Convenient That in all time Coming the Law shall be, that in no Case Whatever a Ball Shall be Lifted without losing a Stroke Except it is in the Scholar's holes When it may be Taken out teed and played with any Iron Club without losing a Stroke—And in all other Cases the Ball must be Played where it lyes Except it is at least half Covered with Water or filth When it may if the Player Chuses be Taken out Teed and Played with any Club upon loosing a Stroke."

The most striking feature of these original Rules is how little, in more than 250 years, the basic idea of the game has changed.

These first Rules also indicate how rugged were the course conditions with which our forebears had to deal.

Article 1, for example, shows how difficult it must have been to hole a short putt!

The original Rules of Golf, rules 1–6.

7. At Holling, you are to play your Ball honestly
not to play upon your Adversary's Ball, not lying

8. If you shoud lose your Ball, by it's being taken
you are to go back to the Spot, where you struck
Ball, and allow your adversary a Stroke for

9. No man at Holling his Ball, is to be allowed, t
Hole with his Club or any thing else. ———

10. If a Ball be stopp'd by any person, Horse, Dog
Ball so stop'd must be played where it lyes. ——

11. If you draw your Club, in order to Strikes & proc
as to be bringing down your Club; If then, your
any way, it is to be accounted a Stroke.

12. He whose Ball lyes farthest from the Hole is

13. Neither Trench, Ditch or Dyke, made for th
the Links, nor the Scholar's Holes or the Solo
accounted a Hazard, But the Ball is to be t
with any Iron Club. ——————— John Rattra

Authentic entry from the Minute Book of the Company of Gentlemen Go
Verification: Encyclopaedia Britannica 15th edition 199

Article 4, which deals with what we would call now "loose impediments," indicates how primitive the playing conditions were and how fragile were the golf clubs.

Article 10 reminds us that there was a great deal of traffic on the links, which were public areas—as the Old Course at St. Andrews still is—when the townspeople engaged in all sorts of activities including "playing at golf, futball…with all other manner of pastimes."

Article 7, directing that the ball "be played honestly for the hole," dictates that golf is not croquet. Nonetheless, playing an adversary's ball in order to knock it away as in croquet was expressly allowed as late as 1814 at Bruntsfields Links.

Article 13 is the first example of what we now call a local rule.

In Article 4, the reference to "fair Green"—the part of the course corresponding to the modern "fairway"—is a reminder that originally the term "The Green" meant the whole playing area of the course. Our modern expressions "Through the Green," "Green Committee," "Green Fee" and "Greenkeeper" derive directly from it.

The Society of St. Andrews Golfers adopted these original Rules in 1754. As the Society evolved into the Royal and Ancient Golf Club of St. Andrews, the Club continued to expand and interpret the Rules.

Eventually, a remarkable development occurred: The Rules promulgated by this private golf club located on the northeast coast of Scotland became accepted as the Rules defining the game for golfers everywhere in the world.

or the Hole, and,

n your way to the Hole.

, or any other way),

ast, & drop another

misfortune

ark his way to the

any thing else, The

so far in the Stroke,

Club shall break in

liged to play first.

reservation of

s Lines, Shall be

en out, and playd

Teed

pt.

, Edinburgh, Scotland, 1745
rinting vol. 28 ©1994

Rules 7–13.

7

1951: Worldwide Joint Rules Conference

Uniform Rules of Golf

THE EVOLUTION OF THE RULES OF GOLF IS an interesting exposition of how good sense can achieve uniformity in an otherwise chaotic situation.

As the game developed in the British Isles, each prominent club had its own rules. In effect, therefore, there were as many different games being played as there were clubs. Good sense, however, recognized not just the value, but the necessity of a uniform set of Rules so that, near the end of the 19th century, requests from a considerable number of clubs caused the Royal and Ancient Golf Club of St. Andrews (R&A) to publish Rules of Golf, which all clubs in the Isles eventually accepted.

A good deal of the spread of the game around the world was in one way or another influenced by British subjects. So the R&A Rules were accepted everywhere but in the United States and Mexico.

When the United States Golf Association (USGA) was formed in 1894, it adopted essentially the R&A Rules as the USGA Rules of Golf. Golfers in Mexico decided to play by the USGA rules.

During the next 50 years, there began to be divergence between the two codes of rules. Sensible and effective leadership took hold of the developing dichotomy. In the spring of 1951, first in London and then in St. Andrews, representatives of the R&A, USGA, Australian Golf Union and the Royal Canadian Golf Association met. Joseph C. Dey, Jr., who was then the USGA's Executive Secretary, described the London meeting:

"For four days those twelve men explored every phase of the Rules. There were no axes to grind, no ultra-nationalistic views. They were just golf lovers and they worked together in complete harmony.

"They reached full agreement on a uniform code. They had a wonderful experience together and a memorable one."

It was more than a memorable experience; it was, in its impact on the development of a single game of golf everywhere in the world, monumental.

The attendees at the Worldwide Rules Conference were (left to right, front row) Dr. James Lawson, R&A; Isaac B. Grainger, chairman of the USGA Rules of Golf Conference; Dr. Harold Gardner-Hill, chairman of R&A Rules of Golf Comm.; Commander J.A.S. Carson, R&A secretary; (back row) J. C. Dey, Jr., USGA executive secretary; I. Whitton, Australian Golf Union; Lt. Col. John Inglis, deputy chairman of R&A Rules Comm.; Richard S. Tufts, USGA secretary; and Colin Rankin, Rules chairman of the Royal Canadian Golf Association.

Inset: *The 1952 Rules of Golf.*

8

1950: Ben Hogan Wins The Open After a Near-Fatal Car Accident

The U.S. Open

THE PHOTOGRAPH OF BEN HOGAN'S FOLLOW-through on his second shot with a 1-iron onto the 72nd green of the 1950 U.S. Open Championship at Merion is probably the most reproduced piece of art in the history of golf.

His classic pose suggests a wonderful golf shot. The situation, moreover, was intensely dramatic, because Ben needed a par 4 on that formidable, 458-yard hole to get into a playoff with Lloyd Mangrum and George Fazio. The moment caught by that photograph was the culmination of a journey which, for ordinary mortals, would have been impossible.

Ben was the son of the village blacksmith in Dublin, Texas. Caddying was his entree into golf. He was no "phenom." What he lacked in stature and weight—he was only 5 foot 8 1/2 inches tall and weighed 135 pounds—he more than made up for with sheer guts, relentless determination and six-hour practice sessions.

In February 1930, Hogan entered the Texas Open at San Antonio as a professional. He was 17. After two rounds, he withdrew. The next week, it was the same story in the Houston Open. He withdrew and went home. He knew that his game was not good enough. He practiced harder. In 1931 and 1932, he made his first serious attempt at the TOUR. He came home flat broke. He tried again in 1934. Again, he came home broke.

In May 1937, he made a third try. He played through the summer, then started for the winter tour. Early in 1938, as he and his wife Valerie drove to Oakland, they were down to their last $85. Before the first round, Ben left his motel room, and found the rear of his car jacked up on cinder blocks, his two rear wheels and tires stolen. Playing "harder than I ever played before or ever will again," he finished third, won $285 and somehow managed to keep going.

In 1940, Ben finally broke through with his first individual TOUR win. He won three more events and ended the year as leading money winner, something he repeated in 1941 and 1942.

After World War II, his game continued to develop, and he went to the pinnacle of the game when he won his first U.S. Open in 1948 at Riviera.

The famous Hy Peskin photograph of Ben Hogan in the final round of the 1950 U.S. Open at Merion.

8 1950: Ben Hogan Wins The Open After a Near-Fatal Car Accident

By February 2, 1949, Hogan was solidly established as one of the premier players of the game. On that morning, he was driving with his wife Valerie to his home in Fort Worth, Texas. Suddenly, a Greyhound bus came out of the fog and hit Hogan's car head-on. Ben probably saved his life as well as Valerie's when he threw himself across the seat to shield her. A split second later, the impact drove the steering column into the now-empty driver's seat.

Ben was brutally injured. While he would live, there was serious doubt that he would ever walk again, much less play golf at any level. That doubt, however, did not take into account what Hogan's courage and determination could accomplish.

In December 1949, eight months after the accident, he played his first round of golf, riding in a golf cart, his legs encased in tight athletic wrappings. In mid-January of the next year, he played in the Los Angeles Open at Riviera, shot 73-69-69-69—280 and tied Sam Snead. Hogan lost the playoff, 72 to 76. As Grantland Rice wrote, "He lost to Snead because his legs just weren't strong enough to carry his heart."

When he came to Merion just five months later in June 1950, the pervading question was: Could Hogan keep his game at the required level for the two rounds played on the final day?

He began with 72-69 to be two shots off the lead after 36 holes. On the final day, a 72 in the morning round left him still two shots back. In the afternoon, he played steady golf, reaching the 12th hole one over par and leading by three strokes. But then, after his tee shot, his legs locked and he limped over to his friend Harry Radix. "Let me lean on you a little bit," he said, then added, "My God, Harry, I don't think I can finish."

Wracked with pain, he three-putted the 12th and the 15th, then failed to get down in two from a bunker at 17. His lead was gone. At the 18th, he somehow managed to put his drive where he needed to be and then played the shot of the championship, the 1-iron into the green. It finished 40 feet from the hole. He two-putted for a 74 and a total of 287 to tie Fazio and Mangrum.

The question then was could his legs carry him for a fifth round. In the playoff, Hogan answered the question decisively, firing at the pins and gunning for birdies. He shot a 69 to beat Mangrum by four shots and Fazio by six.

Hogan's 1-iron was stolen before the playoff. But he did not need it at 18 again. His drive was so long, a smooth 5-iron sufficed.

The 1-iron was recovered in 1982 and now rests in its own glass case at the USGA's museum in Far Hills, New Jersey. The worn-out area on the clubface, about the size of a quarter, is a memorial to how good a ball striker Ben Hogan was.

Ben Hogan is presented the U.S. Open trophy for his victory at Merion. Valerie Hogan shares in the victory.

Inset: *Two months after the near-fatal auto accident, Ben Hogan is transferred from the El Paso Hospital to Fort Worth.*

9

1953: Ben Hogan's 'Triple' in the Majors

The Masters

WHEN BEN HOGAN MADE HIS FIRST START OF the year in 1953, at the Masters, most golf pundits felt that his best years were in the past. His age was against him—he would be 41 on August 13—and then there was his disappointing record in the previous year.

In the 1952 Masters, he had gone into the last round tied with Sam Snead, but finished with a 79, three-putting five times. In the 1952 U.S. Open, he had led after two rounds with a pair of 69s, then finished third with two 74s. By the end of 1953, Ben had demonstrated how fallible the experts can be.

In 1953, he played in only six events. He won five of them, and finished third in the sixth. Three victories were in major championships —The Masters and the U.S. and British Opens. He did not play in the PGA Championship because it was scheduled too soon after the British Open. No one had made his "Triple" before. No one has made it since. Today, it is still the closest achievement to Bobby Jones' Grand Slam of 1930.

In the Masters, he shot a solid 70 in the first round, only two off the pace, despite missing short putts on 17 and 18. His second-round 69 put him in the lead, although he had missed putts from less than five feet on 11, 15 and 16.

His third round of 66 blew away the field, his 54-hole total of 205 breaking Byron Nelson's record by two strokes. That 66 included three-putting twice and missing three short birdie putts! He coasted home with a second 69, winning by five shots. His total of 274 was a record, five better than that set by Ralph Guldahl in 1939. Ben called his performance the "best I have ever played for 72 holes."

Ben Hogan drives off the tee in the 1953 Masters.

9 1953: Ben Hogan's 'Triple' in the Majors

The U.S. Open

The 1953 U.S. Open was played at Oakmont, which had a well-earned reputation for toughness, thanks to its furrowed bunkers and greens so fast that Snead once joked that the coin he used to mark his ball slid off one of them!

In 1927, Tommy Armour's winning total there was 301, and, in 1935, Sam Parks broke 300 by only a stroke. Snead said of Oakmont, "You gotta sneak up on these holes. Iffen you clamber and clank up on 'em, they're liable to turn around and bite you."

Hogan's first round was a five-under 67. But, in the second round, he bogeyed 16 and 18 and took 72. Meanwhile, Snead had shot 72-69, just two shots more. In the third round, Snead led briefly; but then, after driving the 292-yard 17th, he tried too hard for an eagle from 40 feet instead of playing for a sure birdie. The ball rolled nine feet past the cup, and Snead missed the return putt. After 54 holes, Hogan still led by a stroke, 212 to Snead's 213.

With three holes to play, Hogan still held that lead. He finished brilliantly, fading a 2-wood into the 234-yard 16th, driving the green at 17, and placing a 5-iron six feet away on 18. He went 3-3-3 for 71 and a total of 283. Snead was second at 289.

Hogan hits out of the rough at the 1953 U.S. Open at Oakmont. Note the "furrowed" sand in the bunker.

9 1953: Ben Hogan's 'Triple' in the Majors

The British Open

Hogan's year came to a brilliant close at Carnoustie, Scotland with his victory in the British Open, the first and only time he played in the championship. To do it, Hogan had to adapt his game at short notice—from American "target golf" to the bounce-and-run links game, and from the American ball (1.68 inches in diameter) to the then-smaller British ball (1.62). Moreover, he had to do this on a tough par-72 course that measured 7,101 yards from the back tees. The cold, wet weather added considerably to the length and difficulty of the course, especially for Hogan. His near-fatal car accident in 1949 had left him with limited circulation in his legs.

The first day was windy and cold with occasional hail. Despite bogeys on the last three holes, Hogan managed a one-over-par 73, three shots off the pace. On the second day, he was twice drenched with rain, but played solidly. His 71 left him two shots back.

On the 36-hole final day, he had to cope with cold winds and intermittent downpours. He also had the flu and got a shot of penicillin before he began. Still, despite three-putting for a 6 at 17, he shot a fine 70 in the morning, tying for the lead.

In the afternoon, he parred the first four holes. At the fifth, Hogan's approach hit the edge of the green, but kicked off a slope toward the left bunker. It stopped at the edge of the sand, 40 feet from the hole and suspended "on two blades of grass," as he said later. With one foot in the bunker, the other on the bank, he chipped the ball cleanly—and holed it for a birdie. This put him in the lead.

He then birdied the 524-yard sixth with two awesome woods, dropped a 14-footer for a birdie 2 at the 235-yard 13th and holed a 20-foot birdie putt at the last hole, a par four of 448 yards, as the Scotsmen cheered "The Wee Ice Mon" home.

His 68, a course record, gave him a total of 282. He won by four strokes. But, as Britain's most respected golf writer, Bernard Darwin, said, "If he had needed a 64, you were quite certain he could have played a 64!"

If Ben Hogan needed any credentials for admission into the pantheon of golf's great players, he secured them that afternoon in those conditions with that round of 68.

Ben Hogan with the famous claret jug, emblematic of victory in the Open Championship.

Inset: *Hogan at Carnoustie.*

9 1953: Ben Hogan's 'Triple' in the Majors

A Parade Up Broadway!

When he returned to New York, he was given a ticker tape parade, the first for a golfer since Bob Jones returned from England in 1930.

There is an unimpeachable source for a particularly engaging part of the whole story of Ben Hogan's Carnoustie triumph. He had resisted the suggestion that he play in that championship, because he did not think he had anything left to prove and he saw no reason, therefore, to subject himself to Scotland's weather.

It was Valerie who took the initiative to enter him and then persuade him to play. As he mused about having to deal with the weather, Valerie accumulated all of the ointments, hand warmers and other insulators against the weather she could locate.

When Ben saw what Valerie had gathered, he announced, "If that goes, I am not going!" Valerie's response "If that does not go, I am not going" carried the day, and it all went with the two of them.

The home in which they stayed near Carnoustie had a large staff. When Ben returned from the final round, they were lined up in the drive to greet him. Each of the women in turn curtsied and kissed his cheek and each of the men solemnly shook his hand. Each of them, moreover, had put a good luck charm in his golf bag, which each in turn retrieved. That informal ceremony moved Ben to tears.

It was the only time Valerie had seen him cry!

Ben Hogan triumphantly proceeds up the canyons of lower Manhattan.

10

1935: Gene Sarazen's Double Eagle

The Masters

GRANTLAND RICE, THE PREEMINENT SPORTS writer of the time, called Gene Sarazen's 4-wood second shot on the par five 15th hole in the final round of the 1935 Masters "the most thrilling single shot ever played."

That double eagle certainly made golf history, occurring, as it did, in just the second Masters played. News of the stroke—and Sarazen's ultimate victory—reverberated throughout the golfing world and beyond. It single-handedly boosted the status of the Masters to another level and did much to make it one of the game's major championships.

Sarazen had missed the first Masters in 1934—a great disappointment to him—because the week before the tournament he had to leave on an exhibition tour of South America with Joe Kirkwood. In 1935, he made certain that nothing would interfere with his playing in Bobby Jones' event.

Sarazen was anxious to make a good showing, but it was not going to be easy. Jones had invited a strong field that included Horton Smith, the first Masters winner; Craig Wood; Henry Picard; U.S. Open champion Olin Dutra; and Denny Shute.

To make it even more interesting, Jones himself was playing. The golf experts did not give Jones much of a chance because he had been away from tournament golf for four years since his Grand Slam year of 1930—too long, they considered, even for the greatest golfer of that age. The experts were right. Jones tied for 18th place.

Still, Jones was the pre-tournament favorite, Sarazen was next, with Smith, Wood and Dutra slightly behind. Sarazen's practice rounds had been spectacular—65, 67, 72, 67, adding up to 271, 17 strokes under par.

Even though the weather was very cold for April in Georgia, the scoring was hot. Picard, the "Hershey Hurricane," took the first-round lead with a 67. Sarazen shot 68; Wood, 69. On the second day, Picard continued to lead with a 68 for 135. Sarazen had a respectable 71 for 139, Wood a 72 for 141.

In the third round, Wood shot a great 68 during the blustery rainstorms that swept the course. At the end of the day, he led with a 54-hole total of 209, seven under par, and Dutra, after three 70s, was next with 210. Sarazen had a disappointing 73 and was three strokes behind with 212. Picard's 76 put him at 213.

Gene Sarazen in action.

SARAZEN BRIDGE

ERECTED TO COMMEMORATE THE TWENTIETH ANNIVERSARY OF
THE FAMOUS "DOUBLE EAGLE" SCORED BY GENE SARAZEN
ON THIS HOLE, APRIL 7, 1935, WHICH GAINED HIM A TIE
FOR FIRST PLACE WITH CRAIG WOOD AND IN THE PLAY-OFF
WON THE SECOND MASTERS TOURNAMENT.

DEDICATED APRIL 6, 1955

FRANK CHRISTIAN STUDIOS

10

1933: Gene Sarazen's Double Eagle

With the course rain-soaked and the weather near freezing, Wood and Picard teed off some four holes ahead of Sarazen in the final round. Jones also was playing ahead of Sarazen, who was paired with Walter Hagen. Most of the spectators were following Jones or Wood and Picard.

When Sarazen and Hagen were on the 14th hole, a roar reached them from the gallery around the 18th green. Wood evidently had birdied the final hole. As they stood on the 15th tee, the news reached them: Wood had finished with 282.

At that point, Sarazen was still three strokes behind Wood with four holes to play. Hagen turned toward Sarazen and said, "Well, Gene, it looks like it's all over."

Sarazen snapped back, "I don't know. They could drop in from anywhere." That was one of the more prophetic statements anyone has ever made about anything.

On the 15th hole, Sarazen hit a solid drive. As Hagen played his second, Sarazen asked his caddie, nicknamed Stovepipe, what he needed to win.

"To beat Wood?" asked Stovepipe. Sarazen nodded. Hagen started to laugh. "Oh," Stovepipe moaned, looking at Gene's scorecard. "You need four threes, Mister Gene, 3, 3, 3, 3."

Put another way, Sarazen had to birdie three of the last four holes to tie Wood.

When Gene came to his ball, the lie gave him a nasty jolt. It was, as he says, "none too good." He huddled with Stovepipe as to whether to play a 3- or a 4-wood. To get the ball up Gene would have to go with his 4-wood, a new club with a hollow-back sole that enabled it to get down and through the ball.

Gene tore into the shot with every ounce of strength he had. It flew in, he says, on a very low trajectory, no more than 30 feet in the air. Then, it landed on the front of the green, took one hop and started to roll toward the cup. Gene strained to see what was happening.

Then, the small band of spectators at the green let him know the result. They gave a loud shout, and several were jumping up and down. He knew he had holed out in two.

By itself, the double eagle was spectacular enough, but what gave it its ultimate importance was the circumstances in which it was achieved. With one stroke Sarazen had wiped out Wood's entire three-stroke lead.

Now, all he had to do was par in. This he did, tying Wood at 282. The next day, they played off over 36 freezing and rain-drenched holes. Sarazen won by five shots, 71-73—144 to Wood's 74-75—149.

The double eagle capped a brilliant career in tournament golf. Sarazen's win in the 1935 Masters—together with his earlier victories in the 1922 and 1932 U.S. Opens, the 1932 British Open and the 1922, 1923 and 1933 PGA Championships—made him the first golfer to win all four of the modern professional majors.

The bridge leading to the 15th green is named The Sarazen Bridge in honor of Gene's historic double eagle in 1935. Bob Jones and Clifford Roberts congratulate Sarazen at the dedication ceremony.

Arnold lines up the final putt of the 1960 U.S. Open.

11

1960: Arnold Palmer Wins With Final Round 65

The U.S. Open

THE 1960 U.S. OPEN AT CHERRY HILLS featured a confluence of three of golf's monumental figures, each with a chance to win while playing the last two holes.

The first to finish were Jack Nicklaus and Ben Hogan, who were paired together. Nicklaus, then a 20-year-old amateur, failed to get the birdie he needed on 17 and, disappointed, bogeyed 18 to finish by himself in second place with a total of 282. Nicklaus made a mixed impression on Hogan. As Ben said afterward, "I played 36 holes today with a kid who should have won this thing by 10 strokes."

At age 47, Ben Hogan was still convinced that he could win a fifth U.S. Open Championship, something nobody had ever done. Ben had been playing wonderful golf, hitting every one of the 34 previously played greens in regulation, and, as it developed, needed only pars on 17 and 18 to tie Palmer. It was not to be because a wedge into the green at 17, which spun back into the water, resulted in a bogey 6. Completely drained, Hogan hooked his drive into the water on 18, and three putted for a triple-bogey 7.

Finally, there was Arnold Palmer. His heroics had come early in the round. He had birdied six of the first seven holes. Still six under par as he played 17, he only needed two more pars to achieve his target score of 280, which won the championship.

The playing of those final two holes, therefore, had historic consequences. Arnold Palmer took his rightful place on the throne as the game's king and put the finishing touches on one of the first chapters of the Palmer legend.

Ironically, Palmer's play in the first three rounds—72, 71, 72—had given little indication of what was to come. It had left him a frustrating seven strokes behind the leader, Mike Souchak. Palmer had not played badly, but with the low scores by others in the field, he simply had not been able to keep up with the leaders.

Perhaps Palmer's biggest frustration had been his inability to make his trademark boldness pay at Cherry Hills' first hole, a par four of just 346 yards. Considering the thin air a mile above sea level, he reckoned he could drive the green, and possibly eagle or at least birdie the hole. But in the first three rounds, he had failed. In the first round, he had hit into a ditch on the right, taking a double bogey 6. In the second round, he made a bogey 5 and managed just a par in the third, the morning round of the final day.

Then came a lunchtime conversation which is now golf history.

11

1960:
Arnold Palmer Wins
With Final Round 65

Palmer wondered aloud to Bob Rosburg and golf writers Bob Drum and Dan Jenkins what might happen if he did finally drive the first green.

"I might shoot 65. What would that do?" queried Palmer.

Drum replied, "Nothing. You're too far back."

"It would give me 280," Palmer observed. "Doesn't that always win the Open?"

"Yes," laughed Jenkins, "when Hogan shoots it."

As Palmer left the table, Drum joked, "Go on, boy, go make your seven or eight birdies—and shoot 73!"

When you consider how much prophecy there was in that conversation, it takes on metaphysical character. Palmer did indeed drive that first green, his ball bounding through the rough in front and rolling to a stop just 20 feet away. Two putts later, he had his birdie. On the second hole, a 410-yard par four, he made another, holing a run-up from some 10 yards off the green. On the third, also a short par 4, he chipped his second shot 12 inches from the cup for another birdie. On the fourth, 426 yards long, his full wedge stopped 18 feet away; he holed it for another birdie. He parred the par-five fifth hole; but on the sixth hole, a 174-yard par three, he holed a curling 25-footer for another birdie. On the seventh hole, another short par four, he put his wedge shot within six feet of the cup, and holed the putt for yet another birdie. Six birdies in seven holes.

But, at the par-three eighth hole, he suffered a misfortune that would probably have crushed a lesser spirit. His 3-iron just failed to carry the front bunker. He then hit a marvelous sand shot to three feet, but missed the putt and took a bogey 4. He parred the ninth hole, to go out in 30.

Herbert Warren Wind has justly called it "the most explosive stretch of sub-par golf any golfer has produced in the championship." Arnie, however, was mad! "I wanted that 29," he said to Drum and Jenkins, who now had joined him. Drum's reply soon cooled Arnie's anger. "You've just taken the lead," he said. "The rest of the field is falling back, and you're complaining!"

Palmer played the back nine in 35, one birdie and the rest steady pars. Arnold Palmer had arrived at the pinnacle of the game.

To put Palmer's round in perspective, note the records involved.

▶ He came from seven shots behind to win—this was, and still is, the biggest comeback ever;

▶ His 65 tied the final-round record; and

▶ His front-nine 30 tied the low nine-hole record.

That last round in the 1960 Open firmly established the "Palmer Charge" as one of golf's most exciting phenomenons. Earlier that year, Palmer had won the Masters with a come-from-behind finish, birdieing the last two holes to beat Ken Venturi. But the Open, a far more impressive performance, is the one that everyone would always remember. Throughout his prime, no golfer in the lead, no matter how many strokes he was ahead, would feel safe with Palmer in pursuit.

Arnold exalts after sinking the last putt on the final green of the 1960 Open.

Inset: *1960 U.S. Open Champion Arnold Palmer.*

12

1911: USGA Institutes Handicap System

Universal System

ONE OF GOLF'S MORE IMPORTANT DISTINCTIONS is a system that enables players of different skills to compete fairly with each other. Whether you regularly shoot in the 70s or in the high 90s, you can compete on a level playing field with the finest players in the world.

If baseball is your game, it would be utterly futile to face a Randy Johnson fastball. In basketball, can you imagine trying to stop Michael Jordan intent on a slam dunk? Or in football, can you perceive attempting to block Reggie White? But, in golf, thanks to the handicap system, everyone —given a proper handicap— can play on an equal footing with the best of them. In no other sport is this remotely feasible. In golf, you can realize the fantasy of competing head-to-head with the greatest players in the game.

The original concept of handicapping began informally with the Scots, where strokes were allowed in a match to even out the competition. And as early as 1687—over 300 years ago—there were written references to handicapping.

In the earliest days, each local golf club assigned handicaps to its members. However, given differing computational methods, a need for uniformity arose when golfers traveled for interclub matches.

In Great Britain, the first governing authority to establish a nation-wide system was the Ladies Golf Union. In the United States, it was the USGA that formulated the basis of the handicapping system used today at a meeting at the storied Baltusrol Golf Club on October 11, 1911.

That system has continued to grow and evolve. Aided by the personal computer, we now have more than 4,000,000 golfers with USGA handicap indexes in all 50 states.

The wonderful result of all this is that a 10-handicap player from California can get together with a 20-handicap player from Florida at a golf course in Kansas, and compete on equal terms in a four-ball match with Nicklaus and Palmer.

Golf House, the USGA's headquarters in Far Hills, New Jersey.

13

1987: Europe Wins in U.S. for First Time

The Ryder Cup

THE RYDER CUP—THE CONTEST NOW PLAYED every other year between teams from Europe and the USA—has always been a significant golf event. Nevertheless, up until 1987, it had never attracted very much interest in this country because the matches had been so one-sided. Before 1985, the U.S. had won 21 of the matches, tied one, and lost only three.

Looking back, the tide started to turn in 1979, when European golfers were added to what had been a side confined to professionals from Great Britain and Ireland. Jack Nicklaus had been one of the people who had suggested this change to make the matches more competitive. In 1978, Nicklaus had approached British PGA President Lord Derby, saying, "It is vital to widen the selection procedures if the Ryder Cup is to continue to enjoy its past prestige."

Although the Americans had won again in 1979—by 17 points to 11—three final-day singles had ended with 1-up victories. If those matches had swung the other way, it would have ended in a tie. By 1985, the tide had turned decisively when Europe beat the USA 16½ to 11½ at The Belfry in England.

Still, the U.S. had never lost on American soil. When the 1987 Ryder Cup matches were scheduled at Nicklaus' Muirfield Village course, in Columbus, Ohio, with Jack himself the U.S. Captain, only Europe's tough-minded Captain, Tony Jacklin, his team and their most rabid supporters thought that the Americans could lose. On this side of the Atlantic, at least, everyone—golf experts and weekend golfers alike—was certain that the long line of U.S. victories at home would continue.

The start of the first day's play reinforced that view. Curtis Strange and Tom Kite won the opening foursomes, and then Hal Sutton and Dan Pohl won, too. In the third match, when Lanny Wadkins and Larry Mize were 4-up at the turn on British Open champion Nick Faldo and Europe's top player that year, Ian Woosnam, it appeared that the 1987 matches would be a rout.

Then, as one golf writer put it, "A funny thing happened to the Americans on their way to that rout."

Wadkins' game suddenly turned sour, and Faldo and Woosnam won

The opening ceremonies of the 1987 Ryder Cup at Muirfield Village.

Inset: *Action on the 14th hole.*

13
1987: Europe Wins In U.S. for First Time

the match. That win energized the Spaniards, Seve Ballesteros and Jose Maria Olazabal, and they squared the match at 2-2 with a win over Payne Stewart and Larry Nelson.

The afternoon four-ball matches were a disaster for the Americans. They lost all of them, and the Europeans took what turned out to be a decisive 6-2 lead at the end of the first day.

The quality of the golf on that first afternoon had been of the highest order. In the 68 holes played, the Americans made only four bogeys, yet they lost all four matches to the Europeans, who bogeyed just one hole!

On Saturday morning, the Europeans increased their lead by winning two matches, halving one and losing one so that the score was $8\frac{1}{2}$ to $3\frac{1}{2}$ at the start of the afternoon four-ball matches. These matches were split, with each side winning two. Thus, the U.S. took a $10\frac{1}{2}$ to $5\frac{1}{2}$ deficit into the concluding 12 singles matches on Sunday.

The Americans rallied on the final day. With five matches yet to be decided, Europe's lead had been cut to 12-11. But then a European win and a halved match put them ahead again, $13\frac{1}{2}$ to $11\frac{1}{2}$. It was only poetic justice that the deciding point was won by the man who could be called the soul of the European team, Ballesteros, who beat Strange to secure the European victory with $14\frac{1}{2}$ points. The Americans won the next-to-last match, and the final match was halved so that the final score was 15-13.

The history of the Ryder Cup matches since this European victory has shown how important it was. Simply put, the 1987 matches made the Ryder Cup what it is today—one of the most keenly followed of golf's premier events and certainly one of the most hotly contested.

While Samuel Ryder, the English seed merchant who in 1926 donated the solid gold cup for the matches that bears his name, envisioned adding a significant event to golf's world calendar, he could not have envisioned how significant they have become.

The victorious European Ryder Cup team.

Inset: *Captain Tony Jacklin with the Ryder Cup.*

14

1860: The First Open Championship

The British Open

AS THE GAME OF GOLF DEVELOPED IN SCOT-
land in the 19th century, there was, of course, a good deal of spirited
competition, all of it fairly informal.

For example, in 1849, the four leading players of the time held a series
of matches pitting the Dunn brothers, Willie and Jamie, from Musselburgh, against the St. Andrews pair of Allan Robertson and Old
Tom Morris. The matches started at Musselburgh, where the Dunns
prevailed; moved to St. Andrews, where the home team won, tying the
match; and finished at a neutral venue, North Berwick, where Robertson
and Morris won by a single hole after being four down with eight to play.

In 1860, the Prestwick Golf Club, impressed with the desirability of
an annual test to gauge the comparative skills of professional golfers,
started the championship we now know as the British Open Championship. As the championship prize, they put up 30 guineas for a fine red
Morocco Challenge Belt, richly ornamented with massive silver plates
with golfing designs. (The Belt is similar in appearance to those still
given for boxing championships.) The Club stipulated that the Belt was
to become the personal property of anyone winning it three years in a
row, a feat then considered impossible.

Eight professionals entered that first championship, which was played
at Prestwick. The course then consisted of 12 holes with a total length
of 3,799 yards. The longest hole was the first, at 578 yards; the shortest,
the 11th, at 97 yards.

The course was described as "dodging in and out among lofty sandhills. The holes were, for the most part, out of sight when one took
the iron in hand for the approach; for they lay in deep dells among these
sandhills, and you lofted over the intervening mountain of sand, and
there was all this fascinating excitement, as you climbed to the top of it,
in seeing how near the hole your ball might have happened to roll."

The championship play consisted of three rounds over these 12 holes.
The result of that first championship was no surprise. The two best
players in the field, Willie Park, Sr. and Old Tom Morris finished at the
top, separated only by a couple of shots. Both went on to win four
championships apiece. Andrew Strath, who finished third, was no fluke,
either. He was to win the championship in 1865.

The first fairway at old Prestwick runs alongside a railroad line.

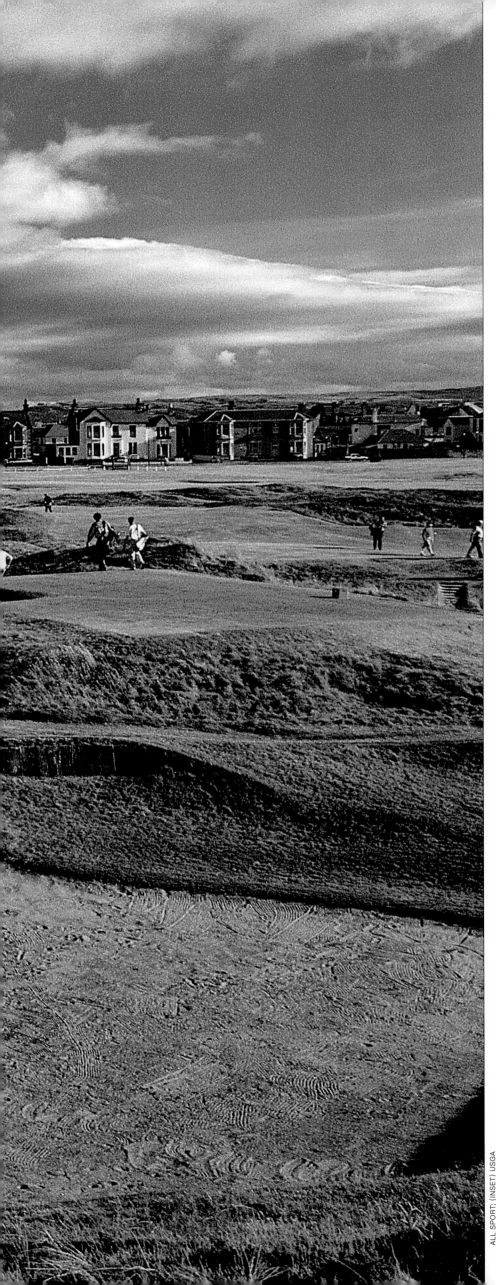

14

1860: The First British Open

The final scores were as follows:

Willie Park, Sr. (Musselburgh)	174
Tom Morris, Sr. (Prestwick)	176
Andrew Strath (St. Andrews)	180
Robert Andrew (Perth)	191
George Brown (Blackheath)	192
Charles Hunter (Prestwick St. Nicholas)	195
Alexander Smith (Bruntsfield)	196
William Steel (Bruntsfield)	232

Strictly speaking, the championship in 1860 was not the first true British Open, because it was for professionals only. However, in a committee meeting of the Prestwick Club on the evening before the second championship, "it was unanimously resolved that the Challenge Belt to be played for to-morrow and on all future occasions until it be otherwise resolved, shall be open to all the world." Although altered conditions—caused principally by the vastly increased number of entrants—have necessitated altered regulations, the Open has, in principle, remained "open to all the world" down to the present day.

Respected Scottish golf historian Robert Browning offers a reason for the change: "Possibly the poor scoring in the 1860 meeting had inspired some of the amateurs with the illusory conviction that they could do every bit as well as the pros."

Be that as it may, Browning is certainly right about the amateurs' "illusory conviction." Up to the present, only three of the finest amateurs of all time have won the championship. The first was Englishman John Ball in 1890—Ball was eight times the British Amateur champion. Second was another Englishman, Harold Hilton, winning in 1892 and 1897. Hilton also won one U.S. and four British Amateurs. The third was arguably the finest amateur ever, the immortal Bobby Jones, who owns the most victories, winning in 1926 and 1927 and again in his Grand Slam year, 1930.

The 18th fairway at old Prestwick, site of the first British Open.

Inset: *Willie Park, winner of the inaugural British Open Championship.*

15

1978: Nancy Lopez Wins Five in a Row

What a Rookie Year!

THE CAREER OF NANCY LOPEZ IS NOT SO MUCH a story as an epic. It began with humble origins, with devoted parents making real sacrifices for their children, and progressed into the development of one of the premier players in the history of women's golf, a lovely person with genuine charm and a warm smile. Her career continues and includes 48 victories on the LPGA Tour.

The humble origins included her father working as a farm laborer and an auto repairman. Nancy's parents somehow managed to finance her golf career by saving small amounts of money each year. On one occasion, they put off buying a dishwasher. On another, instead of buying a larger house, they bought Nancy a car so that she could get to the golf course. The only vacations they took were going to Nancy's tournaments.

Nancy repaid these sacrifices with a stunning career. Born in 1957, she started golf at age 8 under the tutelage of her father, Domingo, and was only 12 when she won the New Mexico Women's Amateur. She then went on to win the U. S. Junior Girls Championship twice (1972 and 1974) and the Western Junior three times (1972-74).

In 1975, she played in the U.S. Women's Open and finished in a tie for second, only four strokes behind the winner. In the following year, she won the AIAW National Championship and Western Amateur. Then, in 1977, she left Tulsa University after her sophomore year to play professional golf. She was just 20 years old.

Any concern over her readiness to play on the LPGA Tour was dispelled by her performance in her first professional event, the U. S. Women's Open, held at Hazeltine National Golf Club in Minnesota. This time she finished by herself in second place, two shots behind Hollis Stacy. She then had three more second-place finishes during the balance of the year.

What she accomplished in 1978, her first full year on the LPGA Tour, would have been extraordinary if she had been a veteran. For a rookie, it was a unique performance.

She won five Tour events in a row—a record unmatched before or since by any other woman player. Later in the year, she won four more

In her rookie year of 1978, Nancy won nine tournaments, including five in a row.

15 1978: Nancy Lopez Wins Five in a Row

tournaments, for a total of nine. Her stroke average of 71.76 won her the Vare Trophy and established a record she bettered herself in 1979 with 71.20. (And that stood as the record until she broke it in 1985 with 70.73.) Besides taking Rookie of the Year honors in 1978, she also was LPGA Player of the Year.

She enhanced the visibility and credibility of the LPGA Tour so as to take its public recognition to another level. Some measure of the impact she made on the world of women's golf during 1978 is provided by her having appeared on the cover of eight major magazines and appearing as a guest on the *Johnny Carson*, *Good Morning America*, *Today* and *Dinah Shore* television shows.

What gives all of that ultimate substance is how she handled her sudden fame. An example is her comment at the time, "I think it's neat that people call me a superstar. It's nice, but I owe everything to my Mom and Dad."

Her career continued to develop. In 1979, she won eight times. Commencing with 1978, with the exception of 1986, she won at least one event every year through 1993. In 1985, she set an all-time record that still stands: at the Henredon Classic she shot a 20-under-par 268 that included 25 birdies. She was inducted into the LPGA Hall of Fame in 1987.

Nancy likes to dedicate her tour victories to those she loves, including her sister and her husband Ray Knight. Now, after 48 victories, her friend Amy Alcott says, "All that's left for Nancy to dedicate a win to is her cat and Uncle Fred!"

Noel Coward once remarked, "Thousands of people have talent. I might just as well congratulate you on having eyes in your head. The one and only thing that counts is: Do you have staying power?"

It can be safely said that Nancy Lopez has staying power.

Although Nancy Lopez has never won the U.S. Women's Open, she came close placing second in 1997.

USGA

16

1982: Tom Watson Edges Jack Nicklaus

The U.S. Open

ONE OF THE MOST MEMORABLE SHOTS IN GOLF history was struck during the 1982 U.S. Open at Pebble Beach when Tom Watson chipped into the cup on the 71st hole, propelling him to a two-stroke victory over Jack Nicklaus.

This Open capped a five-year stretch in which these superstars had fought some classic battles. There was the 1977 Masters, when Nicklaus went into the last round trailing by three strokes. Nicklaus shot a six-under 66, Watson a 67. There was the British Open that same year at Turnberry, when the pair were tied after 36 holes. Paired for the last two rounds, Nicklaus produced 65-66; Watson won with a pair of 65s. Then there was the Masters of 1981, when Watson led Nicklaus by a stroke going into the last round and eventually won by two over him and Johnny Miller.

Even though, for sheer drama, the Open at Pebble Beach had to take the prize, at the start of the championship, neither Watson nor Nicklaus gave any hint of what was to come.

After the first round, the leaders were Bill Rogers, the reigning British Open champion, and Bruce Devlin with two-under-par 70s. Watson had a seesaw round and was tied for eighth, with 72. Nicklaus, with 74, was well back in the pack.

After two rounds, Devlin still led with a 69 for 139. Watson again had an uneven round—two over par going out, two under par coming in—for another 72. Nicklaus was steadier, with three birdies and just one bogey for a 70. They were then tied for eighth at 144.

Overnight rains softened the greens for the third round, and the wind died so that low scores were a real possibility. Watson had taken advantage of the conditions and was tied for the lead with Rogers at 212, four under par. Nicklaus shot a 71 for 215.

Watson had shot a fine 68 with seven birdies and just three bogeys. He said with a smile, "Obviously I like my position. I had a good feeling about my swing, and can't wait for tomorrow. The Open Championship is very important to me, and I'd love to win it on this course."

In contrast, Nicklaus had played steady, but unspectacular, golf with just two birdies and a bogey. Although he continued to hit greens in regulation and be in position for birdies, the putts would not drop. It did

Tom Watson's miraculous pitch from behind the 17th green at Pebble Beach during the fourth round of the 1982 U.S. Open.

16

1982: Tom Watson Edges Jack Nicklaus

not appear to be his Open.

In the fourth round, Nicklaus started badly, failing to get up and down at the first hole, and bogeying it, and then failing to get a birdie at the relatively easy par 5 second. Things looked bleak. The "Golden Bear," however, is never more dangerous than with his back to the wall. From the third hole to the seventh, he ran off five consecutive birdies. This great run put him in a tie for the lead with Rogers, one stroke ahead of Watson.

By the time Watson finished the first nine, he was one stroke ahead of Nicklaus. When Nicklaus birdied the 15th and Watson parred the 13th, they were tied for the lead, and no one else was left to challenge the two preeminent players of the time.

Watson went ahead with a birdie at 14, but then gave it back with a bogey on 16. As Watson approached the 17th tee, he looked at the leader board for the first time that round. His reaction was, "Hot damn, it's just me and Jack!"

Watson hit a good-looking 2-iron off the tee, which started just to the right of the flag, but then started to draw—too much. The ball landed on the left collar and finished in deep rough above the green.

Watson's ball lay some five yards from the hole. When he arrived at the location, he saw that, fortunately, it was sitting up in the grass so that he could slip the leading edge of his sand wedge under the ball. His caddie, Bruce Edwards, said, "Get it close." Watson replied, "I'm not going to get it close, I'm going to make it."

That prophecy turned into a stunning reality. "As soon as it landed on the green, I knew it was in. I just about jumped into the Pacific," Watson said later. As he danced around the green in a display of ecstatic triumph, jumping into the Pacific appeared to be a possibility.

Then, to seal the victory with a flourish, he also birdied 18, for a final-round of 70 and a total of 282, two better than Nicklaus.

Tom's iron out of the rough on the back nine of the final round.

Above: *Tom receives the winner's scroll of the competitors and trophy from President Ford.*

17

1995: Ben Crenshaw's Win for Harvey

The Masters

THE MASTERS OF 1995 BEGAN WITH GREAT media speculation about who might win the year's first major. As Masters week got underway there were many story lines, none involving Ben Crenshaw.

There was the question of whether an American golfer finally could break through European domination of the event. Europeans had won six of the previous seven Masters, seven of the last ten, nine of the last fifteen, including each of the last two.

Then there was the question of whether Nick Price, then Number One in the world rankings and winner of the 1994 British Open and PGA Championship, could win his third major championship in a row.

There also was the story of Davis Love III, who had earned his invitation by winning, in a playoff, at New Orleans, the last TOUR event before the Masters. Would this be the year Love finally won his first major championship?

The media also were intensely interested in a 19-year-old amateur, a Stanford freshman named Eldrick "Tiger" Woods, who would be playing in his first Masters.

The 1995 Masters ended as a major media event, but with a unique story line, one involving a gentle boy who had developed into a gentleman and a teacher who had influenced his life so profoundly. Gentle Ben had been blessed with the loving guidance of a very special golf professional, Harvey Penick, the author of the best-selling *Little Red Book*, who had been teaching him from boyhood.

On the Sunday night before Masters week, Ben learned that Penick had just died at the age of 90. On Wednesday, Ben interrupted his preparation for the tournament and flew home to Austin, Texas, to be a pallbearer at his mentor's funeral. This experience so affected him that, when he returned to Augusta, he could not describe Bud Shrake's eulogy without breaking down. (Shrake was co-author of Penick's *Little Red Book* and others in that series.)

After Ben's opening round 70 and a 67 in the second round, the Harvey Penick-Ben Crenshaw story began to take hold of the Masters. Ben was now tied for fourth, two strokes off the lead. Naturally, the golf writers asked him whether he was trying to "win one for Harvey." Ben's

Ben drives from the tee during the final round.

17 1995: Ben Crenshaw's Win for Harvey

answer was, "I am trying awfully hard. You want to do things like that for someone who has helped you so much, and I'm trying like the dickens."

The "dickens" turned out to be decisive. A 69 in the third round put him in a tie for the lead. A final round of 68, which included birdies on 16 and 17, secured the one-stroke victory.

The scene on the 72nd green was loaded with emotion. After Ben holed the final 18-inch putt, suddenly what had been holding him together gave way completely. He dropped his putter, threw down his cap and, with his face in his hands, began to cry.

"It all let go," he would say later. "I couldn't wait any longer."

What set up this drama had occurred when Ben had visited the ailing Penick two weeks before the Masters. Ben had been putting and playing poorly and asked Harvey for help. Harvey had given Ben his first lesson when he was about six and a half years of age. The old pro now gave Ben, at age 43, one last lesson from his sick-bed.

"Can you please get a putter," Penick asked, "and show me how you're stroking that ball?" Ben did so. "Now I want you to take two good practice strokes," Penick advised. "Then trust yourself and don't let that clubhead get past your hands in the stroke."

As Ben followed this advice, he immediately could feel confidence flowing back into his putting stroke. Later, as the Masters progressed, he observed, "Harvey always said that there's nothing that can boost your confidence in your whole game like holing a couple of putts." And so it proved. Throughout the tournament, Ben's swing as well as his putting stroke appeared grooved and effortless.

The mystical nature of Ben's triumph includes how badly he had played before the Masters and how badly he continued to play afterward. Before, he had not won on the PGA TOUR for a year and had missed three cuts in the four events leading up to the Masters. He has not won since, finishing 23rd on the money list in 1995 and 119th in 1996.

In some way, that transcends understanding. Something was affecting Ben in that magical week. Starting at the moment when he learned of Harvey's death and continuing up to the time when he doubled over on the last green, a strange peace had come over him. He has said, "It was like someone putting their hand on my shoulder and guiding me through."

As Dan Jenkins later wrote in an article for *Golf Digest*, "This Masters was a bad week for atheists."

An emotional Ben Crenshaw reacts to the pressures of the week after the last putt falls in the final round.

Above: *José Maria Olazabal, 1994 Masters winner, places the winner's green jacket on the 1995 Masters champ.*

18

1977: Tom Watson Wins Open Over Jack Nicklaus

The British Open

IN 1977, THE AILSA COURSE AT TURNBERRY, Scotland, was the scene of what could well be described as "The Duel in the Sun." It featured two of the game's superstars, Jack Nicklaus and Tom Watson, and it was something the likes of which no one had seen before, no one has seen since, and no one is ever likely to see again.

For the championship, the course measured 6,875 yards with a nominal par of 35-35—70. However, strict par was 68 since the two par fives were reachable. Even though the seventh (528 yards) did require two big shots, the 17th (500 yards) was only a drive and an iron.

Unfortunately, in the weeks leading up to the British Open, there had been very little rain, and most of the rough failed to grow. To make matters worse, for the four days of the championship the sun was out and there was never much wind—just a firm breeze at most. Without rough or a good, strong wind, the course lost much of its difficulty. Nonetheless, although this was a week when Mark Hayes was to shoot 63 in the second round to set a British Open record, and Watson set a four-round mark eight strokes better than the old, only Watson, Nicklaus and Hubert Green broke par over the four rounds.

In the first round, Nicklaus was out in 37 and home in 31 for a 68. Watson also shot a 68. The leader was John Schroeder with a 66. In the second round, Nicklaus had an up-and-down round, which included three birdies, two three-putts, and a missed eagle putt of eight feet at the 17th. He shot 70. Watson also had a so-so round, and also scored 70. They were now tied at 138, one stroke behind the leader, Roger Maltbie, who faded to a 72-80 in the last two rounds.

In the third round, Nicklaus and Watson were paired together—and the game was on. Nicklaus had four birdies going out to score 31, Watson three birdies and a bogey for 33.

Both birdied 10, but then at the 14th, Nicklaus three-putted, losing a stroke. Watson, now only one behind, got it back with a birdie 2 at the next hole. They then parred in, although threatening to birdie all of the remaining holes. Both shot 65s. This spreadeagled the field—only one other player, Ben Crenshaw, three shots in arrears, could be said to have a realistic chance of winning.

Playing together in the last round, the brilliant play of Nicklaus and Watson soon established that everyone else was playing for third place.

Tom Watson fired a 268 to win the 1977 British Open, beating Jack Nicklaus by one stroke.

18

1977: Tom Watson Wins Open Over Jack Nicklaus

Nicklaus gained two strokes on the first two holes as he scored birdie, par, and Watson failed to get up and down from a difficult place on the second hole. Nicklaus birdied the short fourth to go three ahead, but then Watson got them back with birdies at the fifth, seventh and eighth holes. At the ninth, Watson dropped a stroke to turn in 34 to Nicklaus' 33.

Both parred the 10th and 11th, even though Watson had been forced to hole from five feet at 10 and blast dead from a bunker on 11. Meanwhile, Nicklaus had missed a 12-foot birdie putt for a 2 on 11. At the next hole, Nicklaus holed a 25-foot birdie putt, taking a two-stroke lead with just six holes to play.

However, at the 13th hole, Nicklaus drove into rough and could not pitch close. Watson holed from 12 feet to get one stroke back. He might well have evened the score at the next hole, when he stuck his iron seven feet from the hole. But, uncharacteristically, he missed the putt.

At the 15th, both missed the green with their tee shots, but then Watson took his putter and holed out from at least 60 feet for a birdie, his ball rolling over rough and fringe. Nicklaus could do no better than a 3, so they were now tied.

At the 16th, for one dreadful moment, it appeared that Watson's second was not enough and would roll back into the burn, but it somehow held on the slope, and he pitched the ball dead. Nicklaus was on in two and also got his 4.

Both players hit good drives at the 17th. Watson's iron to the green was excellent, stopping just 15 feet away, but Nicklaus hit his approach "fat," the ball stopping well back from the green. When Nicklaus chipped to five feet and Watson missed his eagle putt, it appeared that Nicklaus would get away with his miscue—but he proceeded to miss the putt. Watson's 4 put him one stroke ahead with one hole to play.

Watson played 18 conservatively, sensibly, driving with a 1-iron right down the middle. Nicklaus decided to gamble with a driver, but hit a nasty slice into deep rough. Watson was away, and hit a brilliant 7-iron, the ball coming to rest just 18 inches from the hole. Somehow, Nicklaus excavated his ball from the high grass and put his second shot on the green, but at least 30 feet from the hole. Incredibly, however, Nicklaus holed his putt for a 3, forcing Watson to hole his 18-incher for the win, which he calmly proceeded to do.

Watson, therefore, had produced another 65 to Nicklaus' 66, and a total of 268 to win by one. Hubert Green finished alone in third place, 10 strokes behind Nicklaus.

These two giants of the game had played a game—effectively a 36-hole match—that will always have an honored place in golf's history. Between them, they were 19 under par for the last 36 holes of the championship, and in the final round, they had a better ball of 30-30—60.

Jack Nicklaus and Tom Watson walk off the 18th green after the second round.

Inset: *It was hard to tell who the winner was after the final round.*

19

1954: Babe Zaharias Wins Despite Cancer

U.S. Women's Open

IN 1954, MILDRED "BABE" ZAHARIAS WON THE U.S. Women's Open Championship despite a bout with cancer. Putting this triumph into perspective requires understanding how extraordinary a person she was.

Born in 1914, she was the daughter of a retired Norwegian ship's carpenter in Port Arthur, Texas; she was one of seven children. Early in her childhood she began to manifest the athletic ability which set her apart from her peers. She loved to run, jump, play baseball, basketball, football, wrestle and box, and learned to do each and all of them better than any boy in her neighborhood. She also became an excellent tennis player, diver, roller-skater and bowler. She got her nickname "Babe" (after Babe Ruth) when she hit five home runs in a baseball game.

At age 18, she entered the 1932 AAU Track and Field Championships with no teammates and yet won the team title. There were 10 events. She entered seven of them and won five, namely the 80-meter hurdles, baseball throw, shot put, broad jump and javelin. She also tied for first in the high jump and was fourth in the discus. In the process, she set three world records.

Two weeks later, in the Olympics, she again won the hurdles and the javelin, setting world records in both.

Later that year, she pitched an inning for the Brooklyn Dodgers in an exhibition game against the Phillies. On another occasion, she struck out Joe DiMaggio.

In 1935, famed sportswriter Grantland Rice, with the perception of a seer, persuaded her to concentrate on golf. While the ultimate results she achieved in the game were phenomenal, they were the product of much painfully hard work. She would practice until her hands became raw, and then managed to go on practicing by soaking her hands in brine and bandaging them.

Starting in 1946 and continuing in 1947, she won 17 consecutive tournaments, which included the 1946 U.S. Women's Amateur Championship. The last win of that streak was the 1947 British Ladies Championship. She was the first American to win the British Ladies since it was first played in 1893, and the first American to win both championships. She won the titles, moreover, in convincing fashion.

Babe lines up a putt en route to her Open championship.

Inset: *Babe waves victoriously to the gallery after defeating Patty Berg in the Serbin Invitation Golf Tournament, her first tournament triumph after her cancer operation.*

19

1954: Babe Zaharias Wins Despite Cancer

In the U. S. Women's Championship at Southern Hills Country Club in Tulsa, her winning margins were 4 and 3, 4 and 3 and 3 and 2 in the semifinals. In the final, she was devastating—holing a 9-iron from 120 yards on the 25th hole for an eagle 2, for example—and won by 11 and 9, the largest margin ever recorded in the championship.

At Gullane, Scotland, in the British Ladies' Championship, she played what Herb Wind called "probably the finest golf of her career." She won her first four matches by 6 and 5, 4 and 2, 6 and 4, and 6 and 5, making one Briton exclaim, "It's cruel to send our girls out against a game like this!" In her next match, despite outdriving her gritty young English opponent by as much as 100 yards, she only won at the 16th hole, but then overpowered her opponents in her final two matches.

In her eight rounds at Gullane, she missed only three fairways. She hit into just three bunkers, holing out from one and leaving herself "gimme" putts on the other two.

She was a very long hitter, averaging 250 yards off the tee, and could dispatch the ball 300 yards when she nailed it. According to Byron Nelson, only half-a-dozen men at that time could hit the ball farther. Asked by the British how she got such tremendous distance on her drives, she replied, "I just loosen my girdle and let the ball have it!"

She turned pro in 1947, led the women's tour in money-winning for four straight years and was a charter member of the LPGA.

In 1953, she was stricken by cancer and underwent an operation, which only delayed the inevitable. Nevertheless, she not only played in the 1954 U. S. Women's Open Championship at Salem Country Club in Peabody, Mass., she thoroughly dominated it.

After the first two rounds, the Babe led by seven strokes on rounds of 72-71—143, one under par. On the morning of the final day, she had increased her lead to 10 after shooting a 73. She finished with a 75 for a total of 291, just three over par. She dropped all three strokes on the last three holes, when she was so far ahead the result was no longer in doubt. At that point she was visibly tired. Her drives, which had been straight down the middle all three days, now sliced and hooked badly.

On the final hole, with the whole gallery gathered around to root her home, she sliced her drive into a dreadful place in the trees. Obviously, the percentage shot was to chip out into the fairway. That was not the Babe's way. She spied a minuscule opening and rifled a long iron through it to the green. It was a masterful shot, and the crowd responded with an ecstatic roar. In the end, she missed her par 4 by an inch, but it hardly mattered. She had finished like a champion.

A short time later the cancer killed her.

Writing in the *New York Herald Tribune*, Al Laney summed up that triumph. "The Babe has now completely outclassed all her challengers. She has set the pattern by which a champion should act on the course and off and in the future all women golfers must be judged as they measure up to the standard or fail to do so."

Babe Didrikson Zaharias after her Open win.

Inset: *Babe with her husband, professional wrestler George Zaharias.*

20

1914: Harry Vardon Wins His Sixth Open

The British Open

TODAY'S GOLFER KNOWS THE "GOLDEN BEAR" (Jack Nicklaus), "The King" (Arnold Palmer) and "The Shark" (Greg Norman). They also appreciate a "Tiger," as in Tiger Woods. But, back at the turn of the century and on up to World War I, another man was known as "The King"—Harry Vardon, aka "The Greyhound."

Besides a total of some 62 career victories, Vardon is still the only player to win six British Opens—in 1896, 1898, 1899, 1903, 1911 and, eighteen years later at age 44, in 1914. His scores of 316, 307, 310, 300, 303 and 306 were made with clubs and balls that were relatively crude and on courses much more rugged than refined.

The rugged conditions of the courses, moreover, were reflected in the rugged behavior of the galleries. As Vardon recalls it, "I wonder if the average golfer has the slightest conception of what a player undergoes…He is battling to win the greatest championship in his profession. Seventy-two holes of medal play is a severe test of skill and nerve to begin with. The addition of an enormous and wild crowd doubles the difficulty. In an effort to have a good view of each stroke, the crowd swarms and surges, and the players are buffeted and knocked about. It may come as a surprise to people to know that, after a big tournament, my ankles and shins are black and blue.(!) The moment I have struck my ball, it is absolutely essential for me to give my club to my caddie to prevent it from being broken by the rushing crowd. As I walk along in the midst of this multitude, I am pushed, elbowed and kicked. (!) Under these circumstances, trying to produce one's best golf calls for incredible concentration and self control."

That latter sentence would appear to be a gross understatement!

Probably Vardon did not have much opposition during those years. Correct? Wrong! It is an odd fact, but great players often come in "threes." In the 60s, it was "The Big Three"—Nicklaus, Palmer and Player. In the 40s, it was Ben Hogan, Sam Snead and Byron Nelson. In Vardon's time, it was "The Great Triumvirate"—Vardon, J. H. Taylor and James Braid. They were almost exact contemporaries—Vardon and Braid were born in 1870, Taylor in 1871. Among them, they won 16 of the 21 Opens from 1894 through 1914.

In 1896, Taylor was the game's top player, having won the two previous

Harry Vardon putting on the fourth green.

Harry Vardon tees off.

1914: Harry Vardon Wins His Sixth Open

Opens. A few weeks before the Open at Muirfield, he met Vardon in a challenge match. Vardon crushed him by 8 and 7. In the Open, a two-day event, 36 holes a day, they tied at 316. (Remember: this was the era of the solid, gutta percha or "gutty" ball, which even top pros could only drive an average of 200 yards.) Vardon won the 36-hole playoff, 157 to 161.

In 1898, Vardon enjoyed his greatest year. He won the Open at Prestwick with a total of 307, shading Willie Park, Jr. by a stroke, and was victorious in so many tournaments—14 in a row, at one point—that Andrew Kirkaldy growled, "That man would break the heart of a stone horse." Taylor muttered, "He's not a man, he's a blooming steam engine."

In 1899, Vardon sucessfully defended his title at Royal St. George's. In glorious weather, he was six strokes ahead after 36 holes with two 76s. On the last day, he shot 81-77 in very strong winds for a total of 310, winning by five strokes. Vardon claimed that his brassie (2-wood) won him the title, saying "I frequently laid the ball dead to the hole with that club."

In 1903, Vardon fell ill. One day, early in the season, he became dizzy and faint. His doctor said it was flu and advised rest. Against his doctor's advice, Vardon traveled to Prestwick for the Open.

Vardon shot a 73 in the first round, tying for the lead. At lunchtime, he had to lie down and rest. He then managed a 77 for 150 to lead by four strokes. The next morning, Vardon felt better and shot a 72, his lead now seven. Afterward, he again had to lie down, and now blood stained his handkerchief when he coughed. He couldn't eat, but drank some Guinness. In the last round, he nearly collapsed, but somehow shot a 78. His total, 300, set an Open record. Harry's brother Tom was second, six strokes behind.

No one knew how ill Vardon was until a little later that year, when he collapsed with a severe hemorrhage. His diagnosis was grim—tuberculosis—and he entered a sanatorium at Mundesley.

However, by February 1904, he had made such good progress that he was allowed to play golf, and he made the only hole-in-one in his life on the Mundesley course. He was discharged at the end of the month.

In 1911, Vardon started a training program, which involved walking 12 miles a day as well as two rounds of golf. Now feeling as fit as ever, Vardon entered the first German Open at Baden-Baden. On a sun-baked course, with ultra-fast greens, he won with 279, the lowest score ever in a major event up to that time.

In the Open at Royal St. George's, Vardon was in second place with two 74s for 148 after two rounds. He had a 75 in the third round for a three-stroke lead, but then lost his rhythm in the afternoon, scoring 80

20 1914: Harry Vardon Wins His Sixth Open

for a total of 303. This allowed the Frenchman, Arnaud Massy, the 1907 Open champion, to tie.

The playoff was anticlimactic. Playing brilliantly, "The Greyhound" raced to a lead of five strokes after 18 holes. The playoff was never completed. On the 35th hole, Vardon holed his putt, and then Massy simply shook Vardon's hand, conceding defeat. (Vardon scored 143 for 35 holes; Massy, 148 for 34.) At 41, Vardon now had five Open titles.

By 1914, all three of "The Great Triumvirate" had five Opens, Taylor winning his fifth in 1913. With war threatening, the trio could sense that this might well be their last chance to win a sixth.

In the first round at Prestwick, Vardon missed several putts on the dry, quick greens, but shot 73 for a one-stroke lead over Braid and Taylor. Missed putts for him and the field were still common in the second round, but his 36-hole total of 150 was good enough for a two-stroke lead over Taylor. (Braid shot 82 and dropped out of contention.)

On the last day, the draw paired the two together. After nine holes, Vardon was three strokes ahead. But at the end of the round, Taylor led by two, having scored 74 to Vardon's 78. By midday, the crowd had grown to 10,000.

In the afternoon, Taylor increased his lead to three at the first hole. On the tee of the third hole, the "Cardinal," then 492 yards long, the loud click of a fan's camera disturbed Taylor at the top of his swing. He mis-hit his shot and took 5. Vardon put his second close to the hole with a brassie and got his 4.

The fourth hole decided the championship. Taylor hit his drive into a bunker, then, still upset by the incident on the previous hole, fluffed his second into the burn and scored 7. Vardon, with his par 4, now took the lead by one.

By the 15th hole, Vardon's lead was five, and although Taylor birdied the 16th to Vardon's bogey, the effort was too late. Vardon parred in for 78; Taylor shot an 83. Vardon's total of 306 left Taylor three strokes behind.

At age 44, Harry Vardon had won his sixth and final Open.

After the championship, Taylor and Braid were the first to congratulate Vardon. That night, "The Great Triumvirate" celebrated the occasion well into the wee hours, toasting 20 years of good-natured rivalry and comradeship.

Vardon was considered quite the swing stylist in his day.

20*

Peter Thomson Wins Fifth Open

The British Open

WHILE HARRY VARDON, TO DATE, IS THE ONLY man to win six British Opens, Australian Peter Thomson and America's Tom Watson have won five each. This puts them in very select company indeed. It is a record only achieved by two others in the history of the championship, namely J. H. Taylor and James Braid, who, with Vardon, formed what golf writers early in this century called "The Great Triumvirate."

Thomson's record also has other unique dimensions. He won three in a row, in 1954, 1955 and 1956, the only man in this century to do so. When he won again in 1958, he established another record: Finishing either first or second for seven consecutive years. He won his fifth Open in 1965.

The first time Thomson finished in the top 10 in the British Open was in 1951 at Portrush, where he tied for sixth place. In 1952, at Royal Lytham and St. Annes, he finished second, one stroke behind South Africa's Bobby Locke, who had also won in 1950. In 1953, at Carnoustie, Ben Hogan was the champion, but again Thomson finished in a tie for second place, four strokes back, with American amateur Frank Stranahan and the Argentinians Antonio Cerda and Roberto De Vicenzo (who was to take the title in 1967).

Thomson's first win came in 1954, the first time that the Open was played at Birkdale. After two rounds, Cerda led with 142, one stroke ahead of Thomson (72-71—143), Welshman Dai Rees and England's Syd Scott. Locke was at 215. All four shot 69 in the third round. In the final round, Scott and Rees finished with 284. Thomson came to 18 needing a 5 for 71 to beat them. Despite being bunkered on his second, he got it. His winning total was 283.

In 1955, Thomson defended his title successfully at St. Andrews. Although the field was rather weak, Th.omson's play was strong; he shot 71-68-70-72—281. After two rounds, Thomson led Bobby Locke, his chief rival, by four strokes, a gap the great South African was unable to close. Australian Kel Nagle, who was to win the British Open in 1960, edging Arnold Palmer by a stroke, and 1954 U. S. Open champion Ed Furgol tied for 19th at 292.

Australian Peter Thomson won his fourth British Open at St. Anne's in England.

20 Peter Thomson Wins Fifth Open

In 1956, Thomson won for the third time in a row at Hoylake. He played great golf, scoring 70-70-72-74—286. A weak entry from America did mar his victory slightly, although many international stars, who had played the week before at Wentworth in the Canada Cup, were there. They included South Africa's Gary Player, De Vicenzo, Cerda, Canadian Al Balding and Australian Bruce Crampton. Thomson won by three from Belgium's Flory Van Donck, with De Vicenzo third at 290 and Player fourth with 291.

Thomson won the British Open for the fourth time at Royal Lytham in 1958. Again, he played excellent golf, shooting 66-72-67-73—278 to tie with Dave Thomas of Wales. The 278 was a record total. Two fine Ryder Cuppers, Eric Brown and Christy O'Connor, were one stroke behind. Thomson won the playoff by 139 to 143.

Golf experts have pointed out that, up to this time, Thomson had not won when all the top Americans were in the field. This cannot be said of his last British Open victory, at Birkdale in 1965.

That year, the top Americans were there. In 1960, Arnold Palmer had played in the British Open for the first time, and won it in 1961 and 1962. Thereafter, the Open had become a "must" for the best U. S. players.

In 1965, Tony Lema was the defending champion. Palmer was back, as was Jack Nicklaus, who had finished second to Lema in 1964. It was a great battle. Lema was off like a rocket, opening with 68. Thomson was six shots back, at 74. But then Lema struggled to a 72 for 140. Palmer was at 141, Thomson, after a 68, at 142, and Nicklaus at 144. Thomson took the lead in the third round with 72 for 214. Lema and Palmer shot 75. Nicklaus had a 77. Thomson's last round was a sound 71. His four-round total of 285 was two shots ahead of O'Connor, and four ahead of Lema.

It was Thomson's last win in the British Open, and his record in the championship had been amazing—five wins, three seconds and 17 top-10 finishes in 20 years.

Peter was, and is, an Australian. His emergence as a dominant player was the harbinger of the end of domination of the game by United States professionals. Gene Sarazen (who at age 56 shot 288 at Royal Lytham and St. Annes) then had a clear perspective on where the game was going:

"American pros used to beat the foreigners' brains out. They still think they can, but, boy, will they get a shock. Australia has plenty more besides Thomson, South Africa has a tremendous group of young players, Britain has some real good ones. There are good players in Italy, Holland, Spain, Belgium, Germany, Argentina and Japan."

Peter Thomson put the initial impetus into that shock wave, which has so profoundly globalized the game.

In 1955 Thomson won his second British Open at St. Andrews.

1929: Joyce Wethered Defeats Glenna Collett

The British Ladies Amateur

THERE ARE SOLID PREMISES FOR ASSERTING that Joyce Wethered was the greatest golfer, man or woman, who ever played the game. One such premise is an appraisal by Bobby Jones who, in his Grand Slam year, 1930, played a round with her at St. Andrews. This is what he said:

"We played the Old Course from the very back, the championship tees, and with a slight breeze blowing off the sea. Miss Wethered…did not miss a shot; she did not even half miss one shot; and when finished, I could not help saying that I had never played golf with anyone, man or woman, amateur or professional, who made me feel so utterly outclassed…It was impossible to expect that Miss Wethered would never miss a shot—but she never did.

"I have no hesitancy in saying that…She is the finest golfer I have ever seen."

Then there is the opinion of Sir Henry Cotton, the three-time British Open champion, who said of her, "In my time no golfer, male or female, has stood out so far ahead of his or her contemporaries…I do not think a golf ball has ever been hit, except perhaps by Harry Vardon, with such a straight flight by any other person."

Miss Wethered's record reinforces these appraisals. The record, moreover, is embellished by her grace and charm.

She conquered the game in a very short time and then moved on to other interests. She played in only 12 championships and won nine of them. She won every one of the five English Ladies Championships (1920 through 1924) that she entered. She won the British Ladies Championship in 1922 and again in 1924 and 1925. She then retired.

The main ingredients of her greatness were said to be her swing, her temperament and, most important, her powers of concentration, which were so extraordinary they were close to being unique.

It is Miss Wethered who is responsible for the "What train?" golf story. In her case, the story is not apocryphal.

In the final of the 1920 English Ladies Championship, she had a putt for the title. As her opponent Mrs. Cecil Leitch, observed, "A long train suddenly rattled by, making the most horrible noise. She appeared quite unbothered by the train, in fact appeared almost in a trance, quite unconscious of any of her immediate surroundings. Later, I asked if the

Joyce Wethered tees off as Glenna Collett looks on.

Inset: *Bob Jones with Joyce Wethered in Atlanta in 1935.*

22

1929: Joyce Wethered Defeats Glenna Collett

train had bothered her. She replied by asking, 'What train?' Remarkable. Utterly remarkable."

While Miss Wethered was dominating British women's golf, an American champion, Glenna Collett, was emerging as the best woman golfer in the United States.

When Miss Collett entered the British Ladies in 1929, Miss Wethered came out of retirement. Although many assumed that Miss Wethered was only competing to respond to the challenge of the great American invader, she denied this, saying that it was the thought of playing in a championship at St. Andrews that had been the deciding factor.

When the draw placed these two titans of the women's game in opposite brackets, the anticipation that they would meet in the final became, to put it mildly, intense. And they did, in an epic 36-hole match.

It is fitting that such a great occasion should have been observed and reported by Bernard Darwin, whose perceptions and pen made him the most respected writer ever to write about the game. He saw the match as divided into four parts.

The first started through the first nine holes, which Miss Collett holed in 34 strokes without making even a hint of a mistake. It lasted for two more holes. By this time Miss Collett had taken 41 strokes to go five up.

News of the match spread like wildfire through the "auld gray toon." A visitor to St. Andrews, not at all interested in golf, who was walking the town to see the cathedral and university, was astonished when a sad-looking mailman on his rounds addressed him with the remark, "She's five doon!"

The second stage of the match was a counterattack by Miss Wethered. On the 12th hole, Miss Wethered had three-putted for a 5, leaving Miss Collett with a three- to four-footer for the win to go 6 up, a near invincible lead. Miss Collett missed and gave Miss Wethered "a ray of hope." On the very next hole, the Englishwoman holed her first good putt of the round and went on to reduce the American's lead to two before lunch.

The third stage featured a brilliant display by Miss Wethered on the first nine in the afternoon, when her score of 35 turned the 2-down deficit into a 4-up advantage.

At this point, Miss Wethered had every reason to believe that, essentially, the match was over. But, then, Miss Wethered later said, Miss Collett gave her a "rude awakening."

Miss Collett began the fourth and last stage of the match by playing the next two holes in three apiece—and winning them both. "This magnificent spurt over the last nine," said Darwin, "was stopped only by Miss Wethered's holing a crucial putt (of 18 feet) on the 15th green to save herself from being pulled down to one."

Miss Wethered went on to win, 3 and 1. She then retired from championship golf again, this time finally, having added yet another dimension to her stature as one of golf's legends.

Joyce Wethered approaching the 14th green at St. Andrews.

Inset: *Miss Wethered with the winners trophy.*

23

1870: Young Tom Morris Wins His Third in a Row

The British Open

THE NAME MORRIS, DISTINGUISHED BY TWO players who bore it more than a century ago, still stands as one of the most important in the history of golf. The two were "Old Tom" Morris and his son, "Young Tom"—also called "Tommy."

Old Tom, and Willie Park, Sr., were undoubtedly the preeminent players of the mid-19th century, winning four British Opens apiece. However, because of his fame as a player and his long association with St. Andrews, the "home of golf," Morris' heavily bearded visage is the one that has become a staple in the photographic history of this era.

Old Tom's accomplishments, however, were only a preface to those achieved by his son in his tragically short life. One can legitimately compare the career of Young Tom to that, say, of Bobby Jones or a Byron Nelson.

In 1866, at 15 years of age, Young Tom played in his first British Open. He took ninth place. In the following year, he won his first pro event and finished fourth in the British Open.

In 1868, he won his first British Open. At 18, he is still the youngest winner. His scores in this championship immediately took the game to a higher level. He won by five strokes, and his total of 154 for the three 12-hole rounds at Prestwick was 13 shots better than that of his father in winning the year before. (Interestingly, Old Tom was 46 when he won in 1867, still the oldest British Open champion.) Young Tom's 154 also demolished Andrew Strath's record, set in 1865, by eight strokes.

In the following year, he won again, his total of 157 putting him in a tie with his father. Tommy won, historians at Prestwick assume, on the strength of a better last 12-hole round, 52 to Old Tom's 53, the first and only time that father and son have tied for the Open as well as the first known win by a matching of scorecards. The pair finished eight strokes ahead of the field.

In evaluating these scores, one must take into consideration how rough was the condition of the course, how crude were the wooden-shafted clubs and solid gutta percha balls of the period, and how much difficulty the wind and weather added. William Doleman, a fine amateur who played in the Opens at that time, later calculated par for Prestwick—on a calm day—at 49. However, as everyone who has played Scottish courses knows, calm days there are the exception rather than the rule!

Old Tom Morris and Young Tom Morris.

USGA

IN MEMORY OF
"TOMMY"
SON OF THOMAS MORRIS
WHO DIED 25TH DECEMBER 1875 AGED 24 YEARS

DEEPLY REGRETTED BY NUMEROUS FRIENDS AND ALL GOLFERS
HE THRICE IN SUCCESSION WON THE CHAMPION'S BELT
AND HELD IT WITHOUT RIVALRY AND YET WITHOUT ENVY
HIS MANY AMIABLE QUALITIES
BEING NO LESS ACKNOWLEDGED THAN HIS GOLFING ACHIEVEMENTS

THIS MONUMENT WAS BEEN ERECTED
BY CONTRIBUTIONS FROM SIXTY GOLFING SOCIETIES

23 1870: Young Tom Morris Wins His Third in a Row

In winning for the third consecutive time in 1870, Young Tom produced the then-phenomenal rounds of 47-51-51 for a total of 149. The players who tied for second place were 12 strokes behind.

Tommy's three consecutive Open victories made the championship belt his personal property. (Later, Old Tom donated the belt to the Royal and Ancient Golf Club of St. Andrews.) It took more than a year to arrange for a new trophy, the silver claret cup still in competition.

There was no championship in 1871.

In 1872, the championship resumed. Again, Young Tom was victorious, scoring 166 in conditions said to be "very adverse to good scoring." He won by three strokes. His four wins in a row is still a British Open record.

One way of illustrating how dominant he was in those years is to note that his average margin of victory was five strokes. Even more impressive, his score of 149 in 1870 is equivalent to an average 18-hole score of 74.5. No one, not even Harry Vardon in his prime, bettered this in the gutta percha ball era. The record stood until 1904, the third British Open played with what we would call a three-piece, wound ball, invented in 1898 by American Coburn Haskell.

In many ways, Young Tom's play reminds one of Arnold Palmer. Like Palmer, he was a broad-shouldered, powerful man. Several times, his steely wrists broke the wooden shafts of his clubs as he waggled. Bold and dashing, he hit the ball a long way and always went for the big carry. Again, like Palmer, he could rip the ball from the worst lies. His iron play was spectacular, and he invented the high pitch with the rut-iron, then a well-lofted club with a fearsomely tiny head. Like Arnie at his best, Tommy was a very bold putter, always running the ball slightly past the hole when it did not fall.

Bernard Darwin once asked Leslie Balfour Melville, the 1895 British Amateur champion who saw Young Tom play, how he compared with Harry Vardon. After a moment's thought, Melville said, "I can't imagine anyone playing better than Tommy did." One might add that Tommy, to make matches more interesting, would often play his own ball against the better ball of two pros or the best ball of three top amateurs—and beat them.

His brief life ended in tragedy. In 1875, his beloved wife of less than a year died in childbirth. Young Tom never recovered from the loss, dying in his sleep a few months later. The official cause of death was a burst artery under the right lung. Unofficially, one can say he died of a broken heart. He was 24.

Tommy was laid to rest in the cathedral churchyard in St. Andrews. On his monument the inscription reads:

"Deeply regretted by numerous friends and all golfers, he thrice in succession won the championship belt and held it without rivalry and yet without envy, his many amiable qualities being no less acknowledged than his golfing achievements."

The memorial to Young Tom Morris in the St. Andrews cemetery.

24

1968: Lee Trevino Wins at Oak Hill

The U.S. Open

THERE ARE THREE FEATURES TO LEE TREVINO'S winning the 1968 U.S. Open at Oak Hill Country Club in Rochester, New York, that made it especially important. First, his score of 275 tied the Open record made by Jack Nicklaus at Baltusrol one year before. Second, Trevino not only broke par in all four rounds, each of his scores—69-68-69-69—was in the sixties. These achievements set two Open records.

The third and, perhaps, the most important feature was the arrival of Lee Buck Trevino at the pinnacle of the game. There is both flair and flavor in the Trevino makeup, which have added a unique dimension to golf's history.

His playing method was also unique: it bore almost no resemblance to a conventional swing. Standing well back from the ball with an open stance, his swing was very flat and truncated. He created the impression that he was "pushing" the ball with the clubhead—it stayed so low and on line so far past impact. Yet, with this seemingly "agricultural" method, as one English golf writer described it, he could hit for considerable distance and with laser-like accuracy.

His very different swing somehow suited his personality. His was one of the more naturally witty and engaging personalities ever to appear on the golf scene.

His humble origins and the manner in which he dealt with them added another element to the Trevino story.

He had been a sergeant in the Marines and went from there to becoming a Texas golf pro chronically short of money. Playing and practicing was his life. He tried to hit 1,000 practice balls every day. When he landed a job as a teaching pro at Horizon City, he and his wife moved into a trailer four miles from the course. Jogging was his primary means of commuting to work.

He played in the 1966 U.S. Open at Olympic Country Club in San Francisco and finished 54th out of the 64 players who made the cut. He earned just $303.

His disappointment over that performance was so acute that he refused to enter the 1967 Open. His wife Claudia, however, did so for him and then persuaded him to try and qualify. To his surprise, he easily qualified at both the local and sectional levels and put himself in the field at Baltusrol. His own description of the start of that experience is worth recording:

Trevino purposefully strides up the fairway at Oak Hill during the 1968 U.S. Open.

Inset: *An exultant Trevino after a birdie putt.*

24

1968: Lee Trevino
Wins at Oak Hill

"I had six shirts, three pairs of slacks and one pair of golf shoes. I never carried a 1-iron or 2-iron then, simply because I couldn't hit any decent shots with them.

"When I walked off the plane at Newark I didn't know where I was going to stay that week. I got into a taxi in front of the airport and asked the driver for some help. He looked me over and figured out I wasn't one of the Rockefellers, so he took me to a little place on Highway 22 called the Union Motel.

"It was strictly small budget, but to me it looked pretty fancy. When you grow up with dirt floors, no plumbing and no electricity, any room that has a television, lights and hot and cold running water is paradise. And the place had a coin laundry. I could take 25 cents and wash everything I had.

"It was my first trip east of the Mississippi River and I didn't have a sports coat or a suit. You had to wear a coat nearly everywhere you went to eat, so I walked about a mile up Highway 22 over a bridge and ate dinner every night at a Chinese restaurant. It was the only place I found where I could go in without a coat.

"It was raining some of the time, so I took my umbrella and sloshed along. I'd get muddy from cars splashing in chuckholes. Then I'd reach the restaurant, eat dinner, drink about 10 beers and have a helluva time getting back to my room. I'm lucky I wasn't killed. They told me Highway 22 was one of the most dangerous roads in New Jersey. Only trouble was, when I got back to my room, I was always starving."

Happily, starvation was a temporary problem, because he shot 72-70-71-70—283, good for fifth place, and won $6,000. His reaction to this was, "Hell, I was the richest Mexican in the world."

That was the catalyst that gave his life a new direction. He became a full-time touring pro and rapidly began to add new dimensions of quality golf and color to the PGA TOUR.

"The $6,000 I won at the Open gave me a little money to go on," he said later. "I decided to try a few more tournaments." The more tournaments he tried, the more he won. In 14 events, he had three top-10 finishes and only failed to make money once.

By the time he reached Oak Hill to play in the 1968 U.S. Open, he had established himself as a player with exceptional ability. His winning by four shots, with no less a player than Jack Nicklaus finishing second, demonstrated that he was going to be a dominant player in the game for a very long time.

Considering his personality along with his talent, it also was clear that the game had been blessed not just with a new superstar, but a unique human being who would put the fun back in golf in much the same way Sir Walter Hagen had done before him. Lee Trevino, soon to be known as the "Merry Mex," was and would be very good, very refreshing, for golf.

1968 Open Champion Lee Trevino.

Inset: *In a famous picture taken in a practice round for the 1971 U.S. Open, which Trevino also won, Lee jokes with a rubber snake.*

25

1973: Johnny Miller's 63 in the Final Round

The U.S. Open

EVERY YEAR AT THE U.S. OPEN, ONE OF THE questions often debated is: What is the greatest single round of golf ever played at an Open? Was it Ben Hogan's closing 67 at Oakland Hills in 1951? Arnold Palmer's last-round 65 at Cherry Hills in 1960? Maybe Jack Nicklaus' 65 in the last round of the 1967 Open at Baltusrol is the one? What about Johnny Miller's 63 in the final round of the 1973 Open at Oakmont?

Certainly, Miller's 63 was the lowest score shot ever shot up to that time in an Open, and it is still the lowest final round. But whether it was the best ever is debatable, because Oakmont's greens, which were "firm and fast" on the first day, in the last three rounds were softer and more receptive.

In the first round, Gary Player took the lead with a 67. After the round, USGA officials planned a five-minute watering of the greens. However, according to a persistent rumor, the watering system malfunctioned, and some greens were watered for an hour or more. The greens were much softer on Friday than on Thursday. As a result, 19 men broke par in the second round.

On Saturday morning, rain fell heavily. When play started at 10:20 a.m., the course was soaked. Oakmont's defenses were seriously compromised.

The low scorer in the third round was Jerry Heard with a 66. He described the round as "like throwing darts. Wherever the ball hit, that's where it stopped."

Meanwhile, Miller shot a 76 in conditions that should have allowed him to make a very low score. As Herb Wind said of him at the time, "Miller is not only an excellent driver, but regularly puts his irons closer to the flag than any other golfer since Byron Nelson." What happened? Miller said he had charted the course earlier in the week and had consulted his notes on every shot of the first two rounds. On Saturday, he simply forgot them!

On Sunday morning, Miller felt so discouraged by that 76 that he told his wife Linda to pack their clothes. They would leave early that evening for the next TOUR event.

He started his final round at 1:36 p.m., nearly an hour before the leaders. At the time, he was six shots off the pace in 13th place.

Miller probably didn't expect much to come of that round, at least

Johnny Miller advances up the fairway with playing partner Miller Barber during the 1973 U.S. Open.

25

1973:
Johnny Miller's 63
In the Final Round

not at first, but an astute observer might have been forewarned by his awesome propensity for low scores; the 61 at Phoenix in 1970, for example, or the 63 earlier in 1973 at the Bob Hope Classic.

Wet as the course still was—heavy humidity had prevented it from drying out—no one should have been too surprised when Johnny stuck his 3-iron five feet from the first hole and made the putt for a birdie. On the second hole, he almost holed his 9-iron, leaving it six inches away. Another birdie. At the third, his 5-iron stopped 25 feet from the flag, and he holed that one for a birdie. At the 549-yard fourth hole, Miller hit a huge drive, but pushed his 3-wood into a greenside bunker. His sand shot spun to a stop three inches from the cup for a tap-in birdie.

After pars on 5, 6 and 7, Miller had his one lapse, a three-putt from 30 feet on the eighth. Then he bounced back with a fine 2-iron at the ninth that settled 40 feet away. Two putts later, he had his birdie 4. He was out in 32.

At the 10th hole, he put his second with a 5-iron 30 feet away, but missed the birdie putt. On the 11th, he hit his wedge from the top of the hill to 14 feet, then holed the putt for a birdie. At the 603-yard 12th, he drove into the rough. He recovered with his 7-iron, then hit a 4-iron to within 15 feet. The birdie putt fell. He was now six under par for the round, three under overall.

Miller kept up his torrid pace. On the 13th hole, he put his 4-iron five feet from the cup, and holed the birdie putt. Now he was tied for the lead with Palmer. At the 14th, Miller had another birdie chance from 12 feet, but missed it by an inch.

The 15th is one of the hardest holes anywhere, a narrow 453-yard par four. Fired up by adrenaline, Miller hit his drive 280 yards, then stuck his 4-iron 10 feet away. He rolled the ball into the center of the hole. He was now eight under par for the round and had taken the lead at five under par.

Now all he had to do was hold on. On the par-three 16th, he hit his 3-wood to 40 feet and two-putted for par. At the 17th, a 1-iron and a wedge to 10 feet gave him another par. On the final hole, he hit his drive 290 yards, then put a 7-iron 20 feet away. His first putt hit the hole, but did not fall. He had his final par.

Out in 32. Back in 31.

His winning total was 279.

The relative softness of the greens has to be considered in evaluating where this peformance belongs among the historic greats. Account also must be taken of how he achieved it. He missed only one fairway. He hit every green but one in regulation and the other, the par-5 ninth, he hit in two. He hit five iron shots inside six feet (two of these within a foot), two more were hit to 10 feet and three others finished 15 feet or less from the hole. He had nine birdies and just one bogey.

When that performance is considered in light of its having been achieved in the last round of the U.S. Open at Oakmont to win by one shot, it certainly has to qualify as historic.

The lithe swing of Johnny Miller, circa 1973.
Inset: *The 1973 U.S. Open champion.*

Afterword

Tiger Woods

Three Boys' Junior Championships, Three U.S. Amateurs and The Masters

THE SELECTION OF THE 25 ACHIEVEMENTS WHICH qualify for consideration as the greatest—described in this book's Foreword—took place before Tiger Woods completed his amateur career and started his PGA TOUR professional career in such spectacular fashion.

As an amateur, Woods compiled a record that, in many respects, is without an equal in golf history. He won the 1991, 1992 and 1993 U.S. Junior Amateurs. Then, in 1994, at the age of 19, he became the youngest winner of the U.S. Amateur. He won again in 1995 and 1996, becoming the first player to win three Amateurs in a row. In 1996, he also won the NCCA championship.

After the 1996 Amateur, Woods announced he was becoming a professional and won two PGA TOUR events before the year was out.

His play in 1997 to date has even been more impressive, with four PGA TOUR wins, including one major championship. At the Masters, Woods won by 12 strokes with 270, breaking the 72-hole record.

Since then he has won the Byron Nelson Classic and the Western Open, his sixth victory in 21 starts.

As of this writing in August 1997, Woods stands atop the TOUR money list with record winnings of nearly $2 million. His stroke average is 68.74.

While there are many more major championships to be won and many more years of superlative play to be accomplished before he can qualify to be in the pantheon of the game's great players, the posssibility of his becoming one of the greats has made his start one of the more exciting developments in the whole history of golf. If that start had occurred while this selection was evolving, it may well have been one of the 25.

Tiger Woods drives at this year's Masters Tournament.

Inset: *(Top) Tiger won the U.S. Junior Amateur Championship in 1991, 1992 and 1993. (Bottom) He also won the U.S. Amateur in 1994, 1995 and 1996.*